DEFENDING IDENTITY

ALSO BY NATAN SHARANSKY

Fear No Evil

The Case for Democracy
with Ron Dermer

DEFENDING
IDENTITY

*Its Indispensable Role
in Protecting Democracy*

NATAN SHARANSKY

with Shira Wolosky Weiss

EDITED BY RON DERMER

PublicAffairs
New York

To our children

CONTENTS

MY ADULT LIFE can be divided into three almost equal parts. First, I was a loyal Soviet citizen, a doublethinker who tried to adapt to and succeed inside a totalitarian regime. Then I became a dissident and ultimately a political prisoner. Finally, since 1986 I have been involved in public and political life in the free world, including almost a decade as a member of parliament and as a cabinet minister in four Israeli governments.

This is my third book, though I never considered myself a writer. I write when I feel that sharing my combined experiences from the dramatically different phases of my life might advance the causes I believe in and help others in their struggle for freedom.

My prison memoir, *Fear No Evil*, was written immediately after my release from nine years in the Gulag. The point of pouring onto paper all the stories from my years as a dissident and a prisoner was to remind everyone—but most of all those who remained trapped behind the iron curtain—how deep are the inner resources that each of us has when we defend our right to be free. I wanted to strengthen the spirits and the hopes of the people left behind.

My second book, *The Case for Democracy*, was written after nearly twenty years in public and political life. In these years the great victory of the free world in the Cold War had been followed by a period when the same free world seemed to want to disarm itself of the most potent weapon in its arsenal: freedom itself. The book was an appeal to democratic political leaders of every party and perspective to appreciate the power of freedom. With the perspective gained from being both a democratic dissident and a politician, I desperately wanted to explain why and how the democratic world can mobilize freedom to overcome the forces of tyranny and terror.

Still, I recognize that the power of freedom alone is insufficient to the task today. For while the democratic world has at its disposal the system that is best able to use the talents and energies of its citizens and as a result has vastly superior material resources, the enemy possesses a strong will.

The enemy's will is strong because his identity is strong. And we must match his strength of purpose with strong identities of our own.

In thinking about the challenges facing the democratic world in building strong identities, I soon discovered that precious few people in the West see identity as a friend of freedom. On the contrary: Identity is regarded by an increasing number of intellectuals and public figures as an antagonist to freedom, as a source of conflict, and as a threat to peace.

Yet the idea of a pitched battle between the forces of freedom and the forces of identity is entirely alien to me. I can read books and articles suggesting it is true. I can hear eloquent rationalizations explaining why it is true. *But I know it is false.* Not only are strong identities vitally important to individuals who hope to lead a life of purpose, they are essential for the ability of a democratic nation to defend its cherished freedoms. Far from being enemies, freedom and identity are staunch allies in the struggle against evil. That is the main message of *Defending Identity*, the message that I believe is important for every individual, every group, and every nation in the free world.

Over time I have come to understand that the notion of identity and democracy as allies is so obvious to me because I had an experience long ago that left an indelible mark on my view of freedom, my view of identity, and my view of the connection between them.

In the books I have written, I have drawn deeply on the experiences of my years in prison. I have done so not because I am under any illusion that the unique circumstances of prison life are easily transferable to the outside world but rather because I believe that those years in the

Gulag afforded me a once-in-a-lifetime laboratory to discover first principles that put a bright spotlight on challenges and confusions that face the world. The lessons of the Gulag are stark but also very clear.

My years in the Gulag convinced me of this powerful alliance between freedom and identity. This is not to say that I never feel any tension between them—only that I recognized long ago that freedom and identity stand on the same side of a great moral divide and nothing I have seen or experienced since has convinced me otherwise. In fact in all my adult life I have doubted this truth for only a single day, and that was many, many years ago—in February 1977. . .

For dissidents in the Soviet Union during the 1960s and 1970s, telephone conversations with their comrades-in-arms abroad were like the light of a lamp on a dark street. It was a joyful reminder that despite all the efforts of the KGB, we were not alone. For me, the unofficial spokesman of two movements—the Jewish immigration movement and the movement for human rights—an important part of my activities took place on the telephone. Speaking very quickly before being disconnected, I dictated appeals from Jewish activists demanding freedom of immigration or Andrei Sakharov's appeals to the president of the United States to press the Soviet regime to release prisoners of conscience. As words from our dissident underground moved to the international stage, I could feel them gaining strength, amplifying the voices of their authors as they traveled across the oceans. And as information trickled back about what was happening in the world's parliaments from friends who had been fighting with us and who were determined to continue our common struggle, we felt that nothing could stop us.

The KGB understood the importance of controlling the lines of communication. That is why there was no direct dialing abroad. Telephone conversations were often jammed, and those telephones that were suspected of being frequently used for "illegal" calls were often simply disconnected. But with inventiveness and stubbornness we would restore our connections, informing our contacts in advance, often through tourists, about where and when and under what name we would be waiting for the next call. And each telephone call brought one more injection of encouragement, energy, and enthusiasm.

Especially precious to me were conversations with my wife, Avital, from whom I had been separated since the day after our marriage. She never abandoned the struggle for our reunion, not even for a single day. But our telephone conversation in the middle of February 1977 was exceptional. After it I felt like a balloon from which the air had been taken out.

It was a difficult time for all the dissidents of the Soviet Union. The Helsinki group created in April 1976 had been publishing dozens of documents about the Soviet Union's failure to fulfill its obligations on human rights under the Helsinki Accords. This had attracted the attention of the entire world. And, exactly as the founders of the group expected, at the beginning of February the repression started. Two leaders of the group, Yuri Orlov and Alexander

Ginsburg, were arrested. A third central figure, Ludmilla
Alexeyeva, was forced to leave the Soviet Union. I, as the
unofficial spokesman of this group, was the next central
activist in line to be arrested. At the same time, the Jewish
immigration movement, which was more massive than any
other dissident group and more specific in its single fundamental demand that Jews should be allowed to leave, was
also under strong attack. For the previous two years we had
established an unbelievable level of international recognition. Official delegations of senators and congressmen were
meeting with us before they went on to summits with Brezh-
nev and other Soviet leaders. In Washington, D.C., our voice
in support of the Jackson Amendment, which linked American trade with freedom of immigration from the USSR,
proved to be stronger than the voice of the Nixon administration, which tried to circumvent it. Direct TV reports,
taped in Moscow, of interviews with refuseniks—Jews who
had been denied exit visas—and coverage of their activity
began to appear on Western screens. (All these events would
later become part of the accusations against me of high treason.) Such obvious and powerful dissident activity bewil-
dered the KGB and in the beginning of the winter they began
their counterattack. Articles and TV programs about Zionist
betrayers of the motherland became more and more threatening. In the official film *Merchants of the Soul,* pictures
were shown of activists and we were called traitors. Searches
and confiscations unprecedented in scale were carried out in
the provinces and later in Moscow. It was clear that all of
this was in preparation for a serious attack against us.

It was at this moment that my conversation with Avital took place. She was calling from Israel. Our words were chosen carefully. There were many things half said, many hints, but the message she was asked to deliver was still very clear. I had to stop my involvement in the Helsinki Watch group and the dissident movements. It was taking me too far. It was dangerous for me and for other Jewish activists. At this critical moment for the entire Jewish movement, it was necessary to be careful. The State of Israel would not be able to defend me if I continued to be at one and the same time both a Zionist and a dissident. It was time for me to separate the two and make my choice between them.

The message was not a new one. I had received it a number of times, in different forms, from Israeli officials. But what made it difficult to simply ignore, as I had done many times before, was that this time the message was sent by them through Avital. What you are saying, I told her, would be a betrayal of the people who have been arrested.

When I met Natalia Steiglitz, later Avital Sharansky, near the Moscow synagogue in October of 1973, it was love at first sight. On July 4, 1974, we had our *chuppah* and the next morning I took her to the airport, where she left with her hard-won exit visa to Israel. We hoped and believed we would soon be reunited there. Throughout the years of separation since then, she had not stopped fighting for our reunion. Even across the vast distance stretching between Russia and the free world, we had always understood each other, even without words. So for her to ask me to do something that I could not do and was not going to do made it seem as if the connection between us, which had been the foundation of my optimism and my strength, was suddenly shaken.

But all this lasted for only twenty-four hours. How Avital succeeded in such a short time to organize another telephone call and to send me a message in Moscow as to where and when I should wait for her call I did not know. But the next evening I heard her voice again. I am sorry, she said; forget everything I told you yesterday. That was a moment of weakness. I fully trust you and I am with you in whatever you do.

Our bond was reestablished and remained unbroken for the next month before my arrest and for the following nine years of my imprisonment. And when we met at the moment of my release in Germany in February 1986, we knew and we felt that we had never been separated.

During all the years of separation, I never knew the details of what had been behind that telephone call. But it was easy to understand the context. My position of simultaneous allegiance to two movements—the struggle of dissidents for freedom and the Zionist struggle for identity—created many suspicions on both sides. Some activists of the Zionist movement and especially Israel officials who were dealing with the question of immigration from the Soviet Union were afraid of my work with Sakharov and other democratic dissidents. My role in the founding of the Helsinki Watch group was viewed as crossing a red line. This was mostly explained by the naïve belief that the KGB was ready to tolerate the struggle for immigration but not ready to tolerate the struggle to fundamentally change the regime. My activities were viewed by some in Israel as creating unnecessary risks to myself and my colleagues in our struggle. What they failed to understand was that to the KGB, any freedom was a fundamental change.

In addition, the Israeli government's attitude was also the expression of a genuine historical concern, based on long and unfortunate experience. Jews had often been ready to fight for many "isms," for freedom across the world, in which they would leave their people, their ghetto, their *shtetl* behind. Communism was only the latest example. But to what good either for the Jews or for the world? Our aim, therefore, should be to go back to our country, to our roots. Leave the abstract struggle for freedom to others: that was their message. The fact that I continued my involvement in both movements looked suspicious to many in the Israeli establishment, even after I had spent nine years in prison for Zionist activity. When I came to Israel I continued to hear insinuations like this: Isn't Sharansky the Soviet version of Timmerman—an Argentine leftist who had been arrested by the junta, was released under pressure from world Jewry, but soon abandoned Israel to join the European world cause?

Many of my colleagues in the human rights movement made the same separation and viewed me with the same distrust. One of the most noble and pure representatives of the Russian intelligentsia, the courageous Lydia Chukovsky, expressed her indignation in a conversation with me during the same difficult period at the beginning of 1977. Why do you have to leave for Israel? Didn't we struggle together for the same ideals? Didn't we share the same beliefs? But now you want to say that you have your own history and your own country, that you have a truth of your own. Another courageous woman, a member of the Helsinki Watch group, Marina Landa, said to me: I am ready to support nationalists only before the victory of their cause. After this victory, they forget about human rights.

Such suspicions continue to follow me. To this day I encounter self-confident democrats who attack me in article after article: When will the real Sharansky stand up—is it the one who is speaking about human rights or the one defending the Zionist state? To my critics, then and now, I had to make a choice: I could fight for universal values or for particularistic values. I could fight for human rights, democracy, and peace or I could fight for the rights of Jews, strengthen Jewish identity, and defend Israel. In this struggle, I would have to choose between the forces of freedom and the forces of identity, between being a man of the world and being a man of my people.

But except for those twenty-four hours between two phone calls with Avital I never felt any problem with my dedication to both; in fact, quite the contrary.

A year later, after my arrest, after accusations against me for high treason, after 110 interrogations, I entered the last stage before my trial, reading the documents prepared by the KGB against me. I spent much time going over the fifteen thousand pages of my "criminal activity," my involvement in both the Jewish movement and the movement for human rights. Suddenly I discovered a film produced in the West after my arrest. Parts of this film had been used as "proof" of my subversive activities.

In the film there was a debate between Ludmilla Alexeyeva, a democratic dissident, and Michael Sherbourn, one of the Zionist activists. They were arguing over why I had been arrested: One said I was arrested as a Zionist, the other, that it had been because of human rights. I could not hold back a smile. The year that had just passed had convinced me more than ever that to the KGB, there was no difference. Both movements were considered enemies. Both posed a threat to KGB control. Both were bulwarks against tyranny.

What I did not know then and could not foresee was that even after the Soviet Union collapsed, this tension would remain. I could not imagine that these two forces, identity and freedom, which were allies in the struggle to resist the world of fear that the Soviets had built, would become the bitterest of enemies in the free world.

DEFENDING IDENTITY

CHAPTER I

Democracy and Identity

IN *The Case for Democracy* I tried to show how the free world has a unique weapon in its hands: freedom itself. The desire for freedom is a powerful force for peace and stability in the world. But as powerful as freedom is in the hearts of men and women everywhere, it is not the only force that moves them. There is another, equally powerful force at work. This is the power contained in identity. Identity is the magnetic force field in which the energies of the world today are moving. It is a force field little understood in the West, but one that influences and even directs events, from the broadest global and international politics to the most local and immediate situations.

The spiritual leader of al Qaeda's declaration that "we will win because the West loves life and we love death," however horrifying and contemptible, offers an insight into the power of identity. He was saying that identity is so precious that it gives him and his Al Qaeda followers something worth dying for. This evil man is correct about one thing, identity is such a powerful force because it opens a world of meaning larger than physical and material life. It asserts that all of life is not merely immediate and that there are things for which life itself is worth sacrificing. By repudiating his words, the free world underestimates the power of its message at great peril.

To the fundamentalists, the West seems shorn of any clear identity, atomized, with each individual living for the day, in pursuit of purely egoistic, materialistic goals. The fundamentalists see a society unwilling to make sacrifices for a cause bigger than the self and view this as a glaring weakness that can be exploited.

What makes matters more ominous is that many in the West seem blithely unaware of the dangers such a lack of identity poses to the values they most deeply cherish. In *Imagine*, his ode to such a utopia, John Lennon conceives of a world without heaven and hell, religion, or nation-states, where there will be "nothing to kill or die for, a brotherhood of man." But a brotherhood without actual brothers, with no one committed to anyone else or to a way of life, is nothing but empty air. It is precisely the vapidness of such meaningless abstractions that encourages Al Qaeda and their ilk to believe that Western values will be swept away in the face of the inexorable power of a community willing to both kill and die for its beliefs.

Those who feel a connection to ideals and values beyond the individual self, who believe that they are participating in a grand collective adventure, and who are convinced that they are acting on behalf of past and future generations are prepared to make great individual sacrifices. This sense of purpose and meaning is what attracts so many to fundamentalism, not only in countries governed by (or torn apart by) fundamentalist groups but even among native-born Europeans. Without a similar strength of purpose and identity, the free world will not long be able to repel the assault against it.

Making the case for identity is much harder than making the case for democracy. No one seriously questions the benefits of a free society. Indeed, we may argue on how best to expand the rule of democracy or how long such an endeavor, if possible, will take, but virtually no one would suggest that a truly free society would not be a boon to its citizens, its neighbors, and the world. The best evidence of the universal respect afforded democracy is that even the world's most undemocratic regimes insist on calling themselves "democratic." Democracy is the motherhood and apple pie of international politics—everyone has to seem to be for it, whatever the differences in backgrounds and recipes.

In contrast, a fiery debate rages in the modern world about the influence of national, religious, and other identities on global peace and stability. This is not merely an esoteric debate among the democratic world's intellectuals, who are themselves preoccupied by post-nationalism, post-modernism, and other post-identity theories. Most people in the West turn on their televisions and see a world seething with hatred based on identity, with daily scenes of terrorism and barbarism that pit national, ethnic, and religious groups against one another. Our newspaper headlines blare day after day that identity groups are attacking and slaughtering one another, from genocidal ethnic warfare in Africa to religious bloodletting in the Middle East. The world sometimes seems an alphabet of disasters: Afghanistan, Bosnia, Chechnya, Darfur; even England is suffering from the threat of ethnic violence, as are France, Germany, Holland. Iraq has revealed the savagery of its internecine forces, and Iran's apocalyptic leadership poses a bewildering array of threats to world peace. It is possible to pursue the catastrophic alphabet all the way to Zambia.

Given this carnage, in which the most terrible atrocities are perpetrated in the name of some sacredly held identity, who could blame anyone for viewing identity as a kind of poison that endangers our world? To many who live in liberal democratic societies, where tolerance is taken for granted, this violence has no rhyme or reason. The struggles appear as a primitivism that recalls the absurdity of the children's story where the world goes to war over which side to butter your bread on. The vicious reality of the conflicts seems to suggest that identity is a force of global destruction, a gun aimed at the head of the free world.

Yet I will argue in this book that while identity can be used destructively, it is a crucial force for good. Strong identities are as valuable to a well-functioning society as they are to secure and committed well-functioning individuals. Just as the advance of democracy is critical to securing international peace and stability, so too is cultivating strong identities. Indeed, only by building societies where both democracy and identity can flourish can we ensure a peaceful world.

What Is Identity?

What is identity? It is not easy to formulate a single definition. Identity can involve a person's connection with history. It can mean the desire to have children be part of this history, to educate them about a valued past so that it becomes part of their future. It could mean belonging to a religious, a national, or an ethnic group.

One universal quality of identity is that it gives life meaning beyond life itself. It offers a connection to a world beyond the self. This can happen by associating with others who share similar backgrounds or religious affiliations, by connecting with previous generations or by being part of a nation or culture. Whatever its form, identity offers a sense of life beyond the physical and material, beyond mere personal existence. It is this sense of a common world that stretches before and beyond the self, of belonging to something greater than the self, that gives strength not only to community but to the individual as well.

Democracy—a free life in a free society—is essential because it satisfies a human yearning to choose one's path, to pursue one's goals. It broadens possibilities and provides opportunity for self-advancement. Identity, a life of commitment, is essential because it satisfies a human longing to become part of something bigger than oneself. It adds layers of meaning to our lives and deepens the human experience. Democracy asserts the value *of* freedom; identity gives a reason *for* freedom. Identity gives freedom purpose, directs it towards a goal, makes it part of a destiny: At stake is not only what your life is like but what your life is for.

Democracy offers a vision of opportunity, self-determination, and peace. But without a particular way of life and a set of commitments to live for, the democratic vision inevitably loses force, becoming empty and abstract. Without identity, a democracy becomes incapable of defending even the values it holds most dear.

Democracy promises and permits various possibilities of self-fulfillment. You are granted the freedom to pursue whatever personal course you choose, to try to attain your ambitions, to live a life fashioned by yourself. Such liberty, if it is to be afforded to all, requires a norm of nonaggression, where no one can impose on others. Freedom in this sense necessitates not interfering with other people's freedom, or as the old saying goes, your freedom ends where my nose begins.

Conceptually, liberal democracy is fundamentally about the individual. Each person is an individual endowed with natural rights who agrees to join with others in a social contract for the benefit of all. The purpose of government, then, is to safeguard those individual rights.

Identity, in contrast, is fundamentally about the links to others. The individual understands himself or herself in terms of a community, not only as a singular independent person but also as an individual attached to others and interdependent with them. Here, identity means identification: solidarity with others with whom you identify. Identity in this sense is a kind of communal self.

This tie to community in the past, the present, and the future is what adds a further dimension to your own immediate activities. It requires that you not simply engage the world as a lone individual. What you do contributes to a larger picture: linking your life to the lives of contemporaries who are part of the same community or to past and future generations of that community. History becomes as Burke described it: a pact between the dead, the living, and the yet unborn. Being part of such a community gives you great strength to defend your values and vision: a strength that comes not only from inside yourself but also in your ties to others who share with you these ideals and who are working to advance them. What you gain is solidarity—the sense of what is common among the members of this mutually committed community, from which each person draws support and strength.

FALSE ENEMIES

Although identity would seem to answer a deep human need for community, building a world in which both democracy and identity can flourish is not easy. To many, democracy and identity are at best suspicious of one another and at worst antagonistic. Each sees the other as opposite and hostile.

For some in the democratic world committed to freedom and human rights, identity means prejudice, intolerance, distrust, and violence against those who are different. Religion and nationalism are negative, even belligerent, words. But for many committed to identity, pure freedom seems egoistic, materialistic, decadent, and weak. The free world's so-called values lack identity's depth of lasting experience and meaning. This contrast is especially felt by those who suddenly enter one of these two worlds. To people who have lived under a totalitarian regime, leaving behind the life of doublethink, where you are afraid to say what you think, is an absolutely exhilarating and liberating experience. This can happen even while you are still living within the borders of the totalitarian world. From the moment you are free to speak your mind, everything looks different. The icons of former belief explode. The great symbols of authority become irrelevant. Appeals to the state, to nationalism, to religion, indeed to any ideology, seem empty. All of these look like prejudices keeping you and so many others from having this liberating experience, this discovery of the free self. It is no surprise that having experienced this liberating feeling, you find yourself a born-again Democrat. Appeals to identity look like a return to the old straightjacket, to that sense of being closed in and pressed down by demands that stifle freedom.

Likewise, for people who have been deprived of a meaningful connection to others, the discovery of a new identity opens a new and larger world that they belong to, one that fulfills and empowers them. Those who find themselves newborn into identity discover the incredible depth of history, the power of belonging, of connecting to past generations and shaping future ones, of living a life that is beyond the self. To them democracy and human rights are meaningful only to the extent that they allow this sense of connection, without which freedom itself can seem empty.

That is why those who discover for themselves one side see the other as unimportant, negligible, if not altogether detrimental. With the exponents of democracy and identity each suspicious of or downright hostile to one another, recognizing and reconciling the virtues of both becomes an exceedingly difficult challenge.

Twice Lucky

I have been extremely lucky—twice lucky in fact. I was deprived of both identity and freedom, and then I discovered them simultaneously. I became a human rights dissident and a Jewish activist almost at the same time, in a way that made one experience reinforce the other, so that each became a source of strength.

The Soviet Union was constructed on an ideology of communism. The leaders of the communist revolution in 1917 spoke of a utopian world where everybody was equal and where exploitation of one by another did not exist. To prevent exploitation, all differences were to be erased. Differences, the Communists said, created injustice and war. Religion, for Karl Marx, was the opiate of the masses, a pretext for exploitation and manipulation. Nationalism was a kind of prejudice used by the bourgeois to organize wars, to exploit the proletariat, distracting their attention from the class struggle. And private property was the most visible expression of this exploitation.

In the name of communist equality, all these prejudices and barriers had to be eradicated. All identities had to be destroyed so that a new identity, based on the solidarity of working people, would be the foundation for a new world where everyone was equal and happy. Decades before John Lennon sung of a world with no nations and religions, Vladimir Lenin worked to build one. Granted, it was understood in the beginning that you would have to remove small groups of class enemies, such as capitalists, who stood in the way of this great dream of equality. But this, Lenin insisted, was a small price to pay for creating a paradise.

In practice, to implement this great ideology, to make this idea succeed, small groups of class enemies soon became large ones. The regime first killed hundreds, then thousands and tens of thousands, then hundreds of thousands, and then millions and tens of millions. But identity dies hard. And the Jews, as I would discover, had some of the strongest identities of all.

I was born in 1948 into this destructive society where tens of millions were killed, deported, exiled to Siberia, starved to death, or thrown into the Gulag. One hundred and fifty million others were controlled by fear, schooled in the arts of doublethink.

I was a typical, assimilated Soviet Jew. Living in a country of doublethink, I behaved like everyone else, acting and speaking like them, trying to suppress any independent thoughts even inside myself. I knew nothing of Jewish religion, history, or culture, or of Israel. Although throughout my youth I had lived in the Ukraine among the killing fields of the Holocaust, I knew nothing about the Holocaust. I knew that some of my relatives had been killed, but not as part of any larger genocide, only as victims of an attack on Soviet Russia.

The only thing Jewish in my life was anti-Semitism. The "fifth-line" of your identity card listing your nationality made sure you never completely forgot your origins. This line brought both restrictions—in studies, in work, in promotions—and suspicions. Being Jewish, therefore, had only a negative connotation. To make life more comfortable, Jews tried to escape into an ivory tower. They could retreat into the world of chess, of science, or of music and bring some measure of security to their lives.

I studied at the prestigious Moscow Institute of Physics and Technology, a place that was far removed from political concerns, which promised an escape into a world of pure ideas and eternal scientific truths. Like many others, I thought of myself as a Soviet citizen, without particular roots or culture. I had no other identity and thus no independent source of strength that might enable me to resist the considerable power of the Soviet state.

Then came a dramatic change: the Six Day War of 1967. Suddenly, Israel had achieved a great victory, and the Soviet regime, which had supplied arms and expertise to Israel's enemies and which had already begun to celebrate Israel's destruction, was utterly humiliated. Intense hatred toward Israel remained, but there was also a begrudging respect, even among the anti-Semites. After all, power was something respected in the communist paradise. Before 1967, to be called a Jew in the Soviet Union was usually to be on the wrong end of an insult. But after 1967, even the jokes about Jews changed to reflect the change in attitude; no longer were they mocked for being cowardly and greedy; now they were criticized for their *chutzpah*.

Even completely assimilated Jews found in this historic moment a new meaning for themselves. Whether they liked it or not, their status in Soviet society was being partially determined by the military triumph of a state thousands of miles away. An identity that we had done nothing to cultivate, that had remained suppressed for generations, and that had brought us only trouble had suddenly reemerged and begun to affect our lives.

It was only then that I started learning about my own Jewish identity. At that moment I understood that I was wrong to think of my history as having begun in 1917 at the founding of the Soviet state. Instead, I started realizing that I was part of a unique history and people that stretched back more than two thousand years, that our ancient Exodus from bondage to freedom was happening in my own generation as well, and that it carried with it a unique message of community, liberty, and hope. And the moment I discovered this connection, this attachment to my history and my people, I discovered an enormous source of strength.

Whereas before, like so many of my generation, I hid in the world of academic science to try to escape the world of lies, now I confronted that world by embracing the truth of my identity. Far from isolating me, this newfound identity would later serve as a bridge to others after I summoned the courage to stop the life of doublethink and reach out to those who had rejected that life as well.

The following year, in 1968, I read in *samizdat* a famous essay by Andrei Sakharov. In this essay he protested the lack of human rights in the Soviet Union and shattered professed notions of Soviet superiority by explaining why the nation's science could not advance without the free exchange of ideas. The foremost scientist in the USSR was risking his privileged life atop the Soviet pyramid to speak the truth. His letter influenced me and many others of my generation. It showed that our efforts to escape the most fundamental moral questions by ensconcing ourselves in an ivory tower would ultimately fail. 1968 was also the year of the Soviet invasion of Czechoslovakia. Seven dissidents went to demonstrate in Red Square—dissidents whose daring we so admired, who had the courage to say what so many of us thought. But still I kept silent.

This silence was broken the day I decided to apply for a visa to emigrate to Israel. It was then that I ended my existence as a loyal Soviet citizen, that I abandoned my life as a "cog," as Stalin put it, in the Soviet regime. Immediately I lost my status, such as it was, in Soviet society. I destroyed my career prospects and many people began avoiding me. But despite the privations, that act of breaking out of the world of doublethink was a wildly liberating experience. Almost simultaneously, two struggles—the struggle for freedom and human rights, and the struggle to recapture my Jewish identity—joined as one experience. From the moment I publicly said what I thought, I gained both freedom and purpose. By fighting for my own right to emigrate to Israel, I was fighting for a basic freedom—the freedom to choose where I would live—and I was fighting also to deepen my connection to my people and my history. Simultaneously, a life of constant self-censorship had ended and a life enriched by identity had begun. Leaving the world of doublethink was like dropping a heavy pack after a long hike: I felt as if I could fly. Reconnecting to my own past was like drinking water after a long fast: I was filling a deep void.

I enjoyed this newfound freedom and identity even under the harsh conditions of a totalitarian regime, even under interrogation, even in the Gulag. The power of these liberating forces was always with me and served as a constant reminder of the difference between my life as a free person with an independent identity and what I had been before. It is this power that enabled me to resist those who sought to break me.

For me, then, the fight for identity and the fight for freedom will be forever intertwined. Identity gave me the strength to become free, and I used this freedom to strengthen my identity still further. Each link I found to the past pulled me further away from the world of fear, and the more I separated myself from this world by speaking the truth that stirred inside me, the more my desire to embrace my own past grew stronger.

Many Jews originally joined the communist revolution because they were determined to work for the benefit of all mankind. They could go beyond their ghetto or *shtetl* and be part of the dream of universal brotherhood, as befitting the descendants of the Hebrew prophets. So they cut off their own roots and joined the Communist Party. But in the end, those who did so helped to build one of the most bloodthirsty regimes in the world, and they found themselves among its first victims.

I discovered that only by embracing who I am—by going back to the *shtetl,* by connecting to my own people, by building my own particular identity—could I also stand with others. Far from negating freedom, identity gave me both inner freedom and the strength to help others. When Jews abandon identity in the pursuit of universal freedom, they end up with neither. Yet when they embrace identity in the name of freedom, as Soviet Jews did in the 1970s, they end up securing both. When freedom and identity are separated, both are weakened. This was the case in the Soviet Union, and this is what threatens to happen in the whole world today.

I wrote this book to make the case for identity. I wrote it to explain why far from being the hostile enemy of democracy, identity is in fact necessary to sustain it. I wrote it to explain why maintaining healthy societies and securing a peaceful world necessitates that identity be framed by democracy and that democracy be anchored by identity. Identity without democracy can become fundamentalist and totalitarian. Democracy without identity can become superficial and meaningless. If either aspect is endangered, we all are endangered. When both are strengthened, we can help secure a more peaceful and meaningful world.

CHAPTER 2

Discovering Identity

The Fear of Death versus the Fear of God

In the Soviet Union, identity and freedom each fought on the same side in a historic struggle against a regime that sought to destroy both. Strong identities, I discovered, were not only a means of deepening and enriching the lives of individuals and communities. They would also prove essential in resisting and ultimately defeating an evil empire. But it was only when I went to prison that I was able to appreciate fully the profound way in which the power of identity, like the power of freedom, is a weapon against tyranny.

When I was arrested, taken to Lefortovo prison, and accused of high treason, I was told I would never get out alive. The choice the KGB put to me was simple. If I cooper-

ated by condemning Israel, Zionism, and the Jewish emigration movement, I would be permitted to join my wife in
Israel relatively quickly. If I refused to cooperate, I would be
executed as a spy and traitor. In choosing the latter, there
would be, I was assured, "no more press conferences." No
one would know about my final days. I would be totally
alone.

The Soviet regime was predicated on controlling, largely
through fear, the minds and the thoughts of hundreds of
millions of people. The existence of even a single person
who does not succumb to fear, who publicly defies it, endangers the entire system. The regime had to crush all signs of
dissent, however small and seemingly insignificant.

"You should not be so stubborn and inflexible," my
interrogators told me. "Cooperate and you will go free.
Let's avoid all the unpleasantness. Declare that we are right
and you are wrong and then you can go on with your life."
In interrogation after interrogation, they repeated the same
sugar-coated threat: "Help us so that we can help you. We
are not bloodthirsty," they purred. "We do not want you to
die. We only want you to cooperate."

This was the typical KGB approach: to make the
moment of your destruction the basis of your release. For
after you have compromised with them, you are no longer a
threat. You are no longer an obstacle in their battle to stamp
out any spark of freedom because you have already sacrificed the most powerful freedom of all: inner freedom. The
KGB does not need your life, only your soul.

In confronting this pressure, I first had to learn to cope
with my own fear, because if my interrogators sensed that I

was afraid, they would surely use it against me. At first, I tried to list all the reasons why I should refuse to collaborate. I started to build a logical case for resistance. I reminded myself that cooperation with the KGB would betray my comrades who were continuing the struggle and weaken my friends working abroad and my wife and family. To cooperate would be to betray the aims of the entire Jewish emigration movement.

But all this logic could not dispel my fear. Why? Hadn't I lived for many years as a dissident troublemaker, a spokesman for outlawed groups who had to deal with KGB tails twenty-four hours a day? Hadn't I risked arrest countless times by raising slogans at demonstrations and passing documents to journalists in front of my KGB tails?

Didn't I know how the regime worked, how far it was willing to go to intimidate opponents, and how serious the charges that could be brought against me? I should have been ready for anything. But my interrogators reminded me again and again that awaiting me was *rasstrel*, execution by firing squad. The word *r-a-s-s-t-r-e-l* pierced my brain like a bullet itself. And under the threat of death, logic begins to break down. Besides, logic never points exclusively in one direction. The same logic that I used to defend myself against the KGB could be used against me. Human beings are inventive. The desire to save one's life is extremely powerful, virtually overwhelming. Moreover, the KGB was expert at turning this desire into a compelling logic of betrayal. In prison, I saw how people desperate to survive invented and accepted the most ludicrous explanations to justify their capitulation and cooperation with the KGB. Collaborators would convince themselves that their actions were rescuing their friends, strengthening their movement, even saving the world.

The logic of betrayal would begin by the KGB reminding you of your personal interests—a young wife, a promising future, and so on—that were needlessly being put at risk. Then they would move from threats to calculated and strategic promises. If you don't sign this letter, they'd warn, they'll have to arrest everybody. But if you sign it, you could "save them" and "prevent their suffering." I recall how one dissident sent a letter to his friends explaining that he had decided to suffer for all of them and that he had negotiated a good deal on their behalf. If there were no dissident publications for three months, he wrote, no one else would be arrested. Another dissident was seduced by the KGB's logic that because he was so extraordinarily clever, he could just pretend to play their game. But in the end, even he couldn't separate the game from reality, and he eventually committed suicide.

Logic, I quickly understood, was not a moral instrument. Instead of being a straight path to truth, logic in the hands of the KGB could easily become a winding road of deception and manipulation. Logical reasons by themselves are not enough to ensure that you are strong enough to resist when facing a death sentence. I soon appreciated that there is a force stronger than the soundest logic that can keep someone from surrendering to evil: the desire to maintain one's inner freedom.

A loyal Soviet citizen was a slave to the system, forced to parrot the ideology of the regime even when he or she ceased to believe it. The moment you broke out of this world of doublethink and began to say what you thought, you became a free person. As long as your thoughts and words were in consonance, you remained free—even in prison. Likewise, the moment you cooperated, the moment you ceased being true to your conscience, you lost your freedom. In effect, you had committed the worst betrayal of all: You had betrayed yourself.

The fire of freedom that burned inside me was fueled by a passionate connection to my people, our common history and our shared destiny. When I crossed the line from doublethink to dissent, I suddenly discovered a new world. I was no longer an isolated Soviet citizen but part of a vibrant community with a long history of struggle and liberation—a history that had left great empires in its wake. I no longer stood alone against a powerful state but rather with my people who were demanding a new Exodus from a present-day tyranny. I stood in solidarity with my fellow Soviet Jews, with Jews in Israel, in America, in Europe, and throughout the world. And the power of this solidarity was nothing less than exhilarating. To cooperate with the KGB would have meant rupturing that solidarity, rejecting that history, and returning once more to a terrible isolation.

Instilling in me this sense of isolation was precisely what the KGB hoped to accomplish during my interrogations. They set out to close me off from my larger world, to destroy my sense of being part of a wider movement, of being part of a cause bigger than myself.

Resistance, I realized, could not just rely on computing logical reasons, but instead meant maintaining a sense of the ties that had given me my powerful sense of inner freedom. I reminded myself that nothing had changed. I had merely been taken two miles from Gorky Street to Lefortovo, placed in the confines of a prison cell, and subjected to interrogators whose goal was to try to make me feel that my whole life did not exist, that they would be the last people to see me alive.

I reminded myself that this was all a lie, that I was still part of the same world, the same struggle, the same history, the same destiny. I remembered the feeling of belonging I shared with others fighting in our common struggle. I told myself again and again that I was now more a part of that world than ever before and more responsible than ever before for the outcome of our struggle. I drew my strength not from logic but from memories of my wife, Avital, my fellow refuseniks, our brave dissident friends. By regaining my ties to others, to a common past, to shared dreams for the future, I was able to pull myself out of the KGB's isolated world into a world of community and belonging. This sense of belonging, this identity, was a reservoir of strength I could draw on to resist.

What became clear from this resistance is that the KGB's method of breaking their victims was to make them focus narrowly on physical survival. Fear for survival, fear of death, ultimately becomes their strongest leverage. If fear overwhelms you, if the desire for physical survival becomes your aim, you are finished. Instead of focusing on your own survival, you must focus on the survival of your people, your history, your culture, and the timeless principles for which you are fighting. The KGB wants you to worry about how to save your own life. You must worry about remaining a free person, true to your convictions and part of a broader world that shares them. You refuse to succumb to the fear of death by refusing to succumb to the fear of being alone in the world. Instead, you think of the values that extend beyond you, of your connection to others, of the vision you share in common. You refuse to go back to being alone. You refuse to go back to being a slave.

At the time of my interrogations, I did not have the right words to describe this feeling of commitment that provided me with such a powerful sense of inner freedom. But some years later, I found a way to express it. A few days before my arrest, an American tourist gave me a small book of Psalms from my wife, along with a letter she had written. In it Avital explained that she had carried the Psalms with her all year, during her travels around the world to fight for my freedom and for the freedom of Soviet Jewry. Now, she wrote, I feel that you should have it so I am sending it to you. Back then, my Hebrew was in no way adequate to read that book. After I was arrested, the book, along with all my other belongings, was confiscated. Then I began to think about the Psalms and about the note from Avital. The book soon took on an almost mystical meaning for me. I started to fight to have it returned, a battle that continued for three years.

I finally received the little book of Psalms with the news that my father had passed away. I tried to read it, but I still understood little. I had to work my way through it slowly, page by page, comparing different lines, trying to recognize patterns and connect words to each other. The first lines I understood were those of Psalm 23: "Although I walk through the valley of death, I fear no evil, for You are with me."

I noticed that in the Psalms, the word *fear* kept appearing. On the one hand, fear was something to be overcome, such as not fearing evil. But as *yirat hashem,* or the *fear of God,* it had a positive connotation. It took me time to understand what this *fear of God* meant. My understanding was at first very vague and uncertain. But at some moment it occurred to me, seeing it many times, that this fear was connected not simply to God the Creator but to the image of God in which man was created. Mankind was created to be worthy of that image and to be true to it. This required me to go forward in an honest and direct way, without compromising principles. This fear, the fear of not being worthy of the divine image, not the fear of death, was what I was most afraid of in my interrogations with the KGB. I was afraid to lose the world of inner freedom I had found, to fail to stay true to my inner self, to no longer conduct myself in a way that was worthy of the divine image.

After a long hunger strike protesting the denial of my right to send letters to my family, there was a period when I was permitted to do so. In one letter to my mother, I formulated for the first time this fear of God as a sort of divine awe and addressed the question of whether possessing such fear required an unequivocal belief in God.

And if you want my opinion on the origins of this fear of God, whether it was bequeathed from on high or was cultivated by man himself through the course of history, this is essentially a question about the source of religion—that is, a question to which there will never be an answer. And while I am well aware how much blood has been spilled over this question and how important it is to so many people, for me it's immaterial. Having realized there is no answer, I am not searching for it. Does it really matter where this religious feeling stems from, whether man in some fashion was able to rise above his physical nature or whether he was created that way? For me, the important thing is that this feeling really exists, that I sense its force and power over me, that it influences my deeds and my life, and that for ten years it has linked me to Avital more concretely than any letters.

To be true to this divine God's image is to assert the dignity of man. To fail to live up to this image is to deny this dignity: to fail to go on a path that is straight and correct, upright and firm, worthy and honest. To give in to the fear the KGB sought to instill in us, the fear for our physical survival, would be to go off this path of dignity and betray our principles out of personal concern. The KGB wanted us to be controlled by physical fear, ultimately the fear of dying. But we had to sublimate this fear into the larger fear of not being up to the task the Creator had assigned man, the fear of not living in the image of God.

Crucially, this was not just a question of being true to myself as a separate individual. It was a question of being true to myself as part of something larger than the self. To maintain a sense of purpose and commitment, to assert my sense of identity, I decided to recite a prayer. But since I didn't know any prayers at the time, I made up one of my own:

> Blessed are you, King of the Universe. Give me the fortune to live with my wife, my love, Avital, in Israel. Give my parents, my wife, and all my family strength to endure all difficulties until we are rejoined. Give me strength, integrity, intelligence, fortune, and patience to go out from this prison to go to Israel, in a way that is honest and worthy.

I recited this prayer each time I was brought for an interrogation. It was my weapon against isolation. If the threat of death was meant to cut me off from community and history, to make me concerned only about myself, my prayer kept me part of the world I most truly belonged to and helped me break through the walls of the prison that surrounded me. My world was not the world of the punishment cell.

SOLIDARITY

In discovering my Jewish identity, I discovered the strength a person draws from being part of a unique history and community. For some, developing such a unique sense of identity suggests excluding those who don't share that identity. But far from cutting me off from others, I found that by deepening my own identity I became connected to others in a more profound way. Instead of dividing me from those in other communities, my identity enabled me to join them in a common struggle.

Before prison, as part of the Helsinki group, the human rights watchdog organization established to ensure that the Soviets abided by the human rights commitments they had made in the Helsinki Accords, I had helped prepare documents in defense of Pentecostals, Catholics, Crimean Tatars, Ukrainians, and many other groups. This work was a natural continuation and expression of my newly found freedom. But it was only in prison that I began to truly appreciate the feeling of solidarity that can develop between those who are deeply committed to their identities. I would learn how even those with vastly different identities—without a sense of a common past or even a shared future—can profoundly inspire one another. I would learn how the deep attachments others feel to their people, traditions, and history resonate with those who feel similar attachments and build mutual respect.

In prison, I first felt this solidarity with the heroes whose inspirational lives leapt from the pages of a library at Lefortovo, the central KGB prison in Moscow. From the time of my arrest until my trial for high treason, I spent sixteen months at Lefortovo. The KGB library there was one of the few distractions permitted, a way to escape a harsh reality. By Soviet standards, the Lefortovo prison library was extraordinary, perhaps the finest library in the entire country.

During Stalin's purges, countless people were killed, including many of the intelligentsia who possessed libraries that were unique treasures of world thought, procured with great care and devotion. These books were distributed among different KGB institutions and eventually found their way to Lefortovo. In prison, the books had gone through purges of their own. As various authors and editors came to be considered enemies of the people, many introductions went missing, pages were torn out, names and comments were deleted, and volumes had disappeared. But the classical texts survived. (Actually, when I returned to Lefortovo nine years later at the end of my imprisonment, many of the books I had voraciously read there had disappeared, apparently for monetary and not ideological reasons—KGB officers had stolen rare editions and classics for their commercial value.)

I had read most of these books before coming to Lefortovo. Yet reading them now was a completely different experience. Before, I had read Homer, Virgil, and the classics of European literature in a detached way, enjoying them out of intellectual curiosity or as part of my general education or for entertainment. I would read them as if I were sitting in a theater observing a play. But now, between interrogations, where the threat of execution constantly hung over my head, I began to see the events in these books from a different perspective. My whole relation to them, and theirs to me, changed. I began to see their struggles in terms of my own experience in prison and the actions of the protagonists in these stories in terms of my own behavior. It started while I was reading a comedy of Aristophanes. At one point, one hero says to another: "Oh you have the vase from Corinth so you're betraying the motherland." Corinth at that time was at war with Athens. I smiled: I myself was being accused of betraying the motherland for the Americans and facing the same absurdity.

But there were also more subtle echoes of my own predicament in these well-known tales. Don Quixote, who in my earlier reading had seemed a comic figure, was transformed into the ultimate dissident, a free person who was determined to pursue his own vision of the world despite everything around him. He was called crazy. His "madness" consisted of imagining that he had inherited the traditions of knighthood. This was his identity, the principle for which he was ready to die. While I could not relate to that particular identity—the Knights, after all, had killed many Jews, especially in the Crusades—his situation seemed to me deeply reflective of the situation of dissidents in the Soviet Union.

The dissidents who challenged the Orwellian world in which we lived were routinely tossed into the madhouse. Among the documents I helped prepare for both human rights and Jewish emigration groups were accounts of these forced hospitalizations. My interrogators denounced these documents as lies and demanded that I disavow them. "What is madness?" they asked rhetorically. "Doesn't it depend," they argued, "on the society you are in? Anyone who departs from the norms of the society is in fact mad." To the KGB, anyone who thought differently from them was an enemy of the state who deserved to be punished and could be suspected of insanity. Truth and falsehood, madness and sanity were turned upside down in their crazy world, a world in which Cervantes's Don Quixote would feel right at home.

Sophocles's Antigone was another fictional character to whom I could suddenly relate. She had violated the law of the state by burying her brother. Her decision to place loyalty to her family above the arbitrary law of a tyrant resonated with our experience in the Soviet Union. In the USSR, the attempt to destroy a person's loyalty to anything besides the state was part and parcel of the regime's rule. They turned friend against friend, brother against brother, even child against parent. A central hero in the Soviet pantheon was Pavlik Morozov, the twelve-year-old boy who had betrayed his own parents, informing on them for hiding wheat to feed the family and watching approvingly as they were arrested. The public aspect was essential. People were required to condemn anyone arrested from their family. Each of the refuseniks confronted this manipulation and twisting of family relationships directly. Many who wanted to emigrate were denied visas on the grounds that they needed permission from parents, even when those requesting visas were grown "children" in their fifties or older. For the parents to grant such permission would be tantamount to publicly defying the regime. Fearful of losing their positions and jobs (which is generally what happened), many parents refused.

Like Socrates, forced by his fellow Athenians to drink poison because he was "corrupting" their youth, many dissidents were arrested for teaching "religious propaganda" to the youth; like Rabelais, we lived in a madhouse world in which KGB tails who followed us did not officially exist, even when they were right next to us; like Odysseus, we were asked to find reservoirs of courage, daring, and boundless curiosity to outweigh the fear of death.

In all these famous stories about conflict, betrayal, and commitment, I felt a deep solidarity with their heroes. They are noble, I thought to myself. They overcame their fears to do what they believed was right, to live according to their ideals. It didn't matter whether these were figures from history or not, whether they had existed or lived only in books. I had the feeling that these characters from different times and countries were completely real as heroes and as allies. I was no longer sitting like a spectator at the theater. I had joined with my heroes in a real battle. Look, they were telling me: Life is wonderful. There are so many things worth living for. But remember, there are also things worth dying for. Stay strong. Be true to us so that you can be true to yourself. We will help you. Together, we will prevail.

What had changed since my first reading of these books? Why did their heroes suddenly come to life in a way they never had before? Before, I had been a person without an identity, without a sense of being part of a greater movement, community, or history. My discovery of my own identity made me feel solidarity with these figures even though they were different from me in every conceivable way—in their language, their culture, their history, their nationality, their religion, their values, and their vision of the world.

They were my partners now not because of their *particular* identities but because of their *strong* identities, because they each had things that were more important to them than their physical existence. At bottom, we all faced the same challenge: to ensure that the fear of death be sublimated to the fear of not being worthy of the divine image, to the fear of not being true to your innermost self. Armed with an identity of my own, I was able to appreciate their commitment to their own identity, to admire their willingness to sacrifice for what they believed, and to be inspired by their example. Their stories reinforced my sense of inner freedom. I felt that I was defending a world of eternal values, and that in defending those values, I was part of a history that sanctified them and a future that would forever champion them.

Then there was Galileo. Galileo had been one of my great childhood heroes and one of the towering giants of the scientific world in which I tried to ensconce myself safely for many years. His was a great and adventurous mind that had defied all past traditions for the sake of his own vision of the cosmos.

But in the Soviet Union, Galileo was co-opted by the KGB. Galileo was useful to my interrogators because he had recanted before the Inquisition, denying Copernicus's discovery that the earth moved on its axis. As a result, he was released from prison to house arrest. "Look at Galileo," the interrogators told me. "He was a great scientist, and he was clever enough to say that he was wrong and that the authorities were right. That way he could continue his life and career. You can do the same. Agree, cooperate, and get on with your life."

I thought to myself: Galileo was one of the world's greatest minds and, despite his confession, on his deathbed he uttered the words, "and yet it moves," showing his continued commitment to the discoveries of science. But four hundred years later, a modern inquisition was using Galileo against me. This historic figure had been mobilized by the KGB precisely because his fear of death had overwhelmed him. True, Galileo's intellectual genius advanced the boundaries of scientific knowledge, and perhaps some years would have gone by before others discovered what he had in the wake of his capitulation. But Galileo's moral failure was eternal. He stood four centuries later on the side of my oppressors, helping maintain their evil empire. A man who dedicated his life to discovering eternal truth was now being used to prop up a world of lies.

If I do the same by cooperating with a modern-day inquisition, I thought, wouldn't I be helping to prop up this world of lies as well? Wouldn't I be another example of capitulation that could be used against others? I would no longer be part of a history of strength, conviction, and courage but rather become part of a history of weakness, betrayal, and cowardice.

Galileo invented the law of gravitation of physical bodies, but in prison I came to believe that a gravitational pull on the human spirit, an interconnection of souls, also exists. Souls interact across time and space. The decisions people make in a difficult hour, the principles they either abide by or abandon in moments of truth, have consequences not just for their own lives but well beyond. Just as the soul of Socrates had been reincarnated millennia later to inspire me and just as the spirit of Antigone had sprung magically to life to strengthen me, so too Galileo's had been summoned to dispirit and weaken me.

Despite what those like the KGB would have us believe, we are not alone. We are never alone. We can stand either in the light or the shadow of those who came before us, and we can choose to shine a light or cast a shadow on all those who come after us. In abiding by our principles in the face of fear, we make humanity's most precious values even more enduring and bequeath a legacy of hope and inspiration. In betraying our ideals in our difficult hours we betray not only ourselves but also all those uncompromising heroes who had bequeathed us their examples.

Our identities open portals to our past and future, making the life we lead so much more meaningful than our mere physical existence. We become a link in a chain that stretches back, out, and forward. By viewing ourselves as part of this chain, we discover a power that can enable us to overcome our fears and remain true to our innermost beliefs. Armed with this power, we have the strength to stand tall, walk straight, and as I so often prayed, live in a way that is honest and worthy.

IDENTITY OF OTHERS

As well as the allies I found in books and history and memory, I sought out trustworthy fellow prisoners. Not all were equally reliable. Invariably, the ones you could count on to be your allies in resisting the KGB were those who possessed strong identities, who shared this fear of not being worthy of the values of their communities, the histories they were born to, what I came to call the desire to be true to the divine image. They could become your partners in resistance, the people you could depend on in your own battle, who would not give in to the KGB, who would be the last to collaborate. In fact, the stronger a prisoner's identity, the greater the likelihood that the KGB would not succeed in destroying him.

The KGB did everything it could think of to create an atmosphere of suspicion and distrust among the prisoners. Dividing and isolating us from one another was central to their methods. In this, the KGB was only applying more rigorously the same tactics that the regime had always used on the entire Soviet population. The regime set out to destroy all associations, all circles that might support a person's identity and system of values—nation, family, religion—leaving only those controlled by the state. They knew that as long as people had their own ties to each other, they could develop relationships outside state control that could form a basis of resistance. So they set out to cut off each person from every possible attachment. The individual would then stand alone against the awesome power of the state.

Religious associations were considered especially dangerous because they are especially binding. People develop a strong sense of commitment when they share a religious faith. But national and ethnic associations also concerned the authorities. All ties beyond the state's control had to be weakened and ultimately eliminated. Then the regime could impose the identity it wanted. In Stalin's era, even innocent student groups such as Moscow University's Brotherhood of Poor Sybarites—some friends who met, drank, and laughed together a few times—were put in prison for ten years.

During interrogations, the KGB set out to sow doubt and to weaken ties with everyone you had been close to and worked with. In my case, they tried to convince me that most of my colleagues had been arrested, that those who were not in prison were actively cooperating with the KGB, that the dissident movement had been destroyed, and that Jewish leaders abroad were afraid to mention my name so as not to be suspected of being connected to espionage. The logic behind the KGB's methods was clear: If a prisoner feels cut off and closed in, there is a greater chance that he or she will cooperate. Before the trial, strength to resist these efforts came to me from knowledge—gained in accidental holes that would unexpectedly open in the wall of KGB control—of Avital's campaigns and her thousands of supporters. I had also built a community of allies from history and from literature. Yet this was largely a world inside my imagination.

The reality of prison life was that, in the end, you discover that the people you could rely on were those who were strong in spirit and strong in identity, not necessarily people who shared your own particular identity or who belonged to the same faith or cause. They could be very different from you, even hostile. In prison, those who had strong identities could prove to be your allies because they occupied territory beyond the reach of the KGB. They would not become informers or provocateurs. They would not collaborate. With them, you could share information, plan mutual protests, and build resistance. Physical fear did not command these dissidents. Whatever their particular identities, each placed it before his own fear of death.

To prevent prisoners from communicating, prison routine was marked by vigilant and elaborate surveillance, as well as strict punishment. Contact between cells was absolutely forbidden, as were collective letters and statements in defense of other prisoners. Careful precautions were taken to make sure political prisoners didn't even see one another as they moved through the prison.

We would defy these rules in all sorts of ways: We talked through drained-out toilets, tapped in Morse code on radiators, shouted from cell to cell, and tried to deliver written messages by hiding them in the exercise yard or in shower rooms or by throwing them over walls. In this way, we could coordinate protests and watch for and denounce specific abuses. If one prisoner was being beaten or harassed, we would all protest with hunger or work strikes. In this way, despite KGB barriers and provocations, prisoners with different identities became trustworthy allies, giving strength to each other to face a common enemy.

I had been familiar with Pentecostal communities from documents the Helsinki Group had published to expose Soviet repression. I had met some of them before my arrest, helping to organize their meetings with Western journalists. The Pentecostals are modest and simple people, whose only wish is to continue their way of life and raise their children in their faith. For centuries they had searched for safe havens, finally moving to the far reaches of eastern Siberia. But even there they were not left alone. The KGB would periodically demand that their spiritual leaders stop teaching their children about their religion and stop taking them to religious gatherings. But the Pentecostals vehemently refused.

For defying the KGB and educating their children about their faith, they were arrested and thrown into prison. They would be released from prison, teach again, and be arrested again. One Pentecostal, a man around seventy-five years old, was told to sign a paper stating that he would no longer teach his faith. He refused. It was the order of God, he told them, that he continue educating his children and his grandchildren. He was imprisoned repeatedly.

In prison, as in the outside world, the Pentecostals were quiet and kept to themselves. But you knew that the KGB would never succeed in turning them into provocateurs. In Perm 35, the camp I was sent to in the Siberian Gulag, there was a Latvian nationalist, Zhanes Skudra. He was probably the shyest prisoner I ever met, a man who seemed afraid of his own shadow. He never raised his voice and rarely participated in public protests. But when the authorities would demand that he participate in an official event meant to demonstrate his loyalty to the regime, he would say to them, in the meekest voice, as if frightened by his own *chutzpa*, "I already have one God and I can't take Lenin as another."

There were numerous examples like this: of people who

would not fight and would not actively protest but would become defiant immediately and unequivocally when it became clear to them that an action would undermine their faith. They possessed the "fear of God" in the purest sense of the term, without philosophical invention, argument, or rationalization.

The political prisoner with whom I became especially close was a devout Orthodox Christian, Volodia Poresh. His Bible had been confiscated, as had my Book of Psalms, and he, like me, had protested with work strikes and hunger strikes to get it back. From time to time, the authorities would give us back these books, but only for short periods. We would try to understand the connection between these and other "gestures of goodwill" that the authorities would show us, and wondered what pressures were being exerted on the regime to make them do it.

One day Volodia and I found ourselves sharing a cell when his Bible and my Psalm book were both returned to us. It was soon after President Reagan had declared that year, 1983, the "Year of the Bible." We cheerfully started reading sections from our texts to one another, calling our ecumenical studies "Reagan's Readings." We would read one chapter from the Old Testament and one from the New.

I perceived these texts very differently than Volodia did. I could not put aside or forget the ways in which the New Testament has been used as a basis for persecution and hatred against Jews. When we would come to a passage such as, "His blood will be on us and our children," which had been interpreted for ages to mean that the Jews are damned and cursed for supposedly crucifying Christ, I thought of all the innocent Jewish blood that had been spilled over the centuries.

Volodia had brought to prison typical anti-Semitic prejudices. For example, he believed that the world was run by Jews and that at least twenty-five million Jews were in the Soviet Union (there were only a little more than a tenth of that number). But the solidarity of free people true to their identity influenced him, too, and he was glad to change his preconceived opinions. Now he recognized and sympathized with how this text appeared to me from my point of view as a Jew. "I feel that persecuting Jews in the name of Christianity," he said to me, "is the same as murdering one's parents for the sake of affirming a 'new truth.' There can be no justification for this." I wanted Volodia to be strong in his identity and he wanted me to be strong in mine, because it was the best guarantee that we could rely on one another and that we could be friends, allies, and comrades-in-arms.

Our mutual interest against the KGB and the recognition that those we could rely on in this struggle were those who were strong in identity built true understanding, tolerance, and respect. It was not a mutual respect that people champion in the abstract but jettison at difficult moments. It was a mutual respect forged in precisely those difficult moments.

Strong identities made people reliable partners against the regime. That partnership made people respect each others' values. No matter how different our beliefs, we valued strong identities because we knew that they helped those who possessed them defy evil. We knew they gave them the power to remain true to themselves, to "fear God" more than death, to walk in an honest and worthy way.

We lived the golden rule: Do not do to others what you would not have done to you. You don't want the KGB to succeed in weakening you, so don't help the KGB succeed in weakening your neighbor. Although we each had come to prison along separate paths, our trust in one another built bridges across our differences. We came to feel that despite our differences, we had a strong spiritual connection, that ultimately we were each praying to the same God—a God that we prayed would strengthen all of us.

None set out to defend the other's goals. Each was acting out of his own interest. What was most important to each of us was to defend our own identity, not that of others. But we recognized that our mutual struggle against a common enemy necessitated that our allies needed to be as strong in their identities as we were in ours. Despite our profound differences, we recognized that to successfully defend the values most dear to us, we had to make sure that others were strong enough to defend theirs.

So out of a passion for our own identity grew a passion for democracy. For it was obvious to all of us that only in a society where no one is punished for expressing their views could everyone uphold and live true to his or her own identity. If each dreamt of a world where he could express his own views and strengthen his identity without fear, then that world had to be one in which others were allowed to express themselves and strengthen their identities.

At this point, one might argue that the world is not a Soviet prison, that the lessons learned there have little application for the real world. But just as the scientist conducts rigidly controlled experiments in extreme environments to determine fundamental principles, so too life in prison removes the sound and fury of our lives and focuses the mind on fundamentals.

Most people may indeed never appreciate that they ultimately have a stake in ensuring that those of different communities, ethnicities, nationalities, and faiths remain strong in their identities. In the free world, we often see these "others" as a threat. But this is because most of us have never seen a world where freedom has been snuffed out, a world so horrible that our smaller differences pale in comparison to the common threat. What the Gulag taught me was that in confronting such a threat, my greatest allies in defending the things I hold most sacred are those who have the capacity to hold other things sacred.

When I left that Gulag after nine long years, it was crystal clear to me that the power of both freedom and identity had given me the strength to prevail.

CHAPTER 3

The Assault on Identity

GOOD IDENTITY/BAD IDENTITY

In the autumn of 2004, a recently elected member of the Dutch Parliament asked to meet with me to discuss Israeli strategies for integrating new immigrants. Israel has particular expertise in this field, with more immigrants than any country in the world as a percentage of the population. Born in Somalia and having lived in Ethiopia, she was very interested in Israel's absorption of Ethiopian Jews, an ancient community of Jews, most of whom were brought to Israel en masse in 1984 and 1990.

Israel and Europe are deeply connected historically, economically, and culturally, so there is much common ground. However, many European leaders tend to be unsympathetic to Israel's point of view. They mistakenly tend to see Israel through a colonialist lens, believing that our "colonial" problem could be solved, like they believed theirs were, by simply ceding territory. It is hard for them to appreciate the fact that unlike them, Israel was facing an existential, not a territorial, conflict.

But this politician was different. She was sympathetic to Israel's unique security dilemma and, even more uncharacteristically, keenly aware of the importance of combating anti-Semitism in Europe. She understood the dangers of Muslim extremism—how it begins with Jews but then extends to more and more groups, employing greater and greater violence. She was exceptionally articulate and thoughtful.

We really connected, save for one thing: my bodyguards. Like all Israeli ministers, I was provided twenty-four-hour protection, a policy strictly enforced since 2001, when Rehavam Zeevi, an Israeli minister, was gunned down in a Jerusalem hotel room by Palestinian terrorists. On her way out of my office she remarked, "Isn't it awful for you to live this way."

She returned to Holland. A week later, I read in the papers that this exceptional woman, Ayaan Hirsi Ali, had been forced underground. She had been whisked off to a safe house and was being guarded by security teams around the clock, totally isolated and without any communication with the outside world. Theo Van Gogh, with whom she had made a film criticizing Islamic practices regarding women, had been assassinated in the streets of Amsterdam by a Dutch Muslim. He was shot eight times, his throat was slit, and pinned to his body with a knife was a note stating that Ayaan was next. The next time I met her in Holland she was under a security regimen much more severe than mine. Following a controversy over her own immigration to Holland, she was deprived of Dutch citizenship and has since moved to the United States, where she remains under twenty-four-hour protection.

Hirsi Ali's case is only one of many where fanaticism has come to the heart of Europe. How is it possible that European capitals have become a theater for Middle East–style extremism? And what does this confrontation tell us about the struggle between democracy and identity?

Europe is now a storm of clashing currents, a maelstrom of conflicting trends. On the one side, Europe has lost confidence in its own identity, in part in reaction to its own history of war and colonialism. The desire to repudiate this history has led to a vision of pure democracy freed from particular attachments, which are seen to have been the primary impetus for conflict and war. On the other side, the huge influx of immigrants, originally the labor force for an aging Europe, possess strong national, ethnic, and increasingly religious identities. These groups have values and self-definitions that seem alien to—or perhaps even incompatible with—European democratic traditions. In effect, a bitter conflict between democracy and identity is raging in Europe: one side imagines democracy without identity; the other, identity without democracy.

This opposition between democracy and identity is both mistaken and extremely dangerous. Identity without democracy is totalitarian; democracy without identity is weak and self-betraying. Rather than being implacably opposed to each other, democracy and identity demand one another.

The democratic world's rejection of identity has a long history. The dream of transcending differences between people, of removing all borders, of eliminating all divisions that are largely seen as the basis of war and conflicts is an old one. But in modern history, this dream has emerged with new vitality and momentum. There have been two major ideological assaults on identity as the cause of hostility between peoples. The first is Marxism, which dates from the middle of the nineteenth century. The second assault comes from the various expressions of post-identity—postnationalism, post-modernism, multiculturalism—that arose in reaction to the world wars in the first half of the twentieth century.

These two movements are different in many ways, to the point of seeming almost opposites. Marxism offers a universal absolutist approach and a specific goal of a classless society. Post-identity, in contrast, tends to be deeply relativist. Marxism is political; post-identity is cultural. Nevertheless, these two ostensibly different movements share a critical feature in common: They both deny and attack identity. They both also have a sliding scale of condemnation: some identities are much worse than others. In both movements, there are identities that play some positive role in advancing mankind to the desired destination, and there are identities that push this goal further away. Some identities are deemed progressive, others reactionary; colonial and anticolonial; historical and unhistorical—or as Marx put it, "nations with history and nations without history." So some identities are "bad" and others "good."

THE MARXIST ASSAULT ON IDENTITY

Marxist-Leninism was the only permitted ideology in the Soviet Union. It was studied in school, in universities, and afterwards, throughout your life. Between my interrogations, the KGB officials assigned to my case would hurriedly try to study their *conspekt,* the notes from their evening courses in ideological studies. There they were shown how everything happening in the world could and should be explained by Marxist-Leninist ideology.

But life is complicated and full of turbulence. Things change very quickly. One day, Tito and Mao are hailed as progressive leaders; the next they are denounced as dictators. India, Uganda, and Indonesia were at times the leaders of anticolonial movements and at other times the lackeys of American imperialism. The theory of Marxism-Leninism could illuminate these patterns. They could always explain yesterday, but they could never predict tomorrow.

Once I asked the teacher of my required course in social science, with half hidden irony: How do we know exactly when Iraqi patriots turn into extreme nationalists? When do Indonesian anticolonial fighters become militant religious fanatics? But the teacher did not hesitate with his answer. It is so simple, he said. All nations and religions and other movements belong to the transitional period on the way to the classless society. So if they are helping to advance communism, they are progressive. The moment they work against it, they are reactionary. This cynical, utilitarian approach was a foundation of Marxism-Leninism.

Marx connected three powerful sources of thought: the centuries' long dream of a utopian state where everybody would be equal; the link between the structure of the economy and class struggle; and Hegel's dialectic as the form of historical progress. The three combined in Marx's grand analysis of all of human history, of its goals and its meaning:

> The history of all hitherto existing society is the history of class struggle. Freeman and slave, patrician and plebeian, lord and serf, guildmaster and journeyman: oppressor and oppressed stood in constant opposition, carrying on uninterrupted combat, sometimes beneath the surface and sometimes openly, that each time ended either in revolutionary reconstitution of society at large or in the common ruin of the contending classes.

The movement from one historical stage to the other, first from slavery to feudalism and then from feudalism to capitalism, is progressive. And capitalism has its place in this march of progress. As the last stage, it broadens and strengthens its presence both by capturing new territories and colonies and through the improvement of technology in the industrial revolution. This encourages and helps in the development of the proletariat, which comes to include a larger and larger part of mankind. The capitalist lust for profit will then dig its own grave. The proletarians, who have nothing to lose but their chains, will ultimately overthrow capitalism and create a classless society throughout the world. The proletarians will be victorious, and communism—the society where everybody gives according to his abilities and receives according to his needs—will prevail.

For Marx and his followers, nationalism and other differences of identity only draw attention away from the main highway of history, the struggle of the classes.

> The nationality of the worker is neither French nor English nor German; it is labor, free slavery, self-huckstering. His government is neither French nor English nor German; it is capital. His native air is neither French nor English nor German but factory air. The land belonging to him is neither French nor English nor German; it lies a few feet beneath the ground.

Until communism is achieved, mankind is a work-in-process. Within the period of transition, however, everything that accelerates the movement of history is progressive. Everything that holds it back is reactionary. Therefore Marx and Engels, practically from the first day they began working together at the time of the revolutions of 1848, introduced the notion of "nations with history" and "nations without history." Historical nations were England, France, and Germany, which had a developed class structure and a national bourgeois. These nations were extending their powers by conquering colonies, thereby forcing historically undeveloped people, from the Czechs and Bulgarians in Europe to the peoples of Africa and Latin America, into the pathways of "progress." By broadening the world market, they were accelerating the development of the proletariat and as a result bringing the victory of communism closer.

In this struggle to accelerate world revolution, there was no place for political correctness. Here is how Friedrich Engels described the merits of the French conquest of Algeria in 1848:

> And if we may regret that the liberty of the Bedouins of the desert has been destroyed, we must not forget that these same Bedouins were a nation of robbers . . . All these nations of free barbarians look very proud, noble and glorious at a distance, but only come near them and you will find that they, as well as the more civilized nations, are ruled by the lust of gain, and only employ ruder and more cruel means. And after all, the modern bourgeois with civilization, industry, order, and at least relative enlightenment following him, is preferable to the feudal lord or to the marauding robber, with the barbarian state of society to which they belong.

Not only did reactionary classes but whole reactionary peoples have to be destroyed in the movement toward history's fulfillment. In the *Communist Manifesto,* Marx called not only for the "abolition of the family" but also to "abolish countries and nationality." "Workingmen have no country," he wrote, adding that: "National differences and antagonisms between peoples are vanishing gradually from day to day . . . the supremacy of the proletariat will cause them to vanish still faster." "The proletariat must constitute itself *the* nation." Engels was even more specific. National groups were for him "ethnic trash."

> There is no land in Europe that does not contain in some place one or more ruins of nations. Left over from an earlier occupation, pressed back and subjugated by that nation which later became the carrier of historical development. As Hegel said, these nations mercilessly crushed underfoot, were one of the actions of history. These Volkerabfalle became in every instance and remained up until their complete extermination or denationalization the fanatic carriers of counterrevolution. Generally, already their entire existence is a protest against a great historical revolution.

According to Jewish tradition, on the Day of Judgment, or what Jews call Yom Kippur, God decides which individuals will live and which will die. But Marx and Engels were even more powerful; they decided which *peoples* would live and which would die.

If Western Europe, accelerated by the revolutions of 1848, was moving into developed capitalism, Russia remained feudal. For both Marx and Engels, Russia was the most retrograde nation because it hadn't even entered into the capitalist stage of history. In their schematic, Russia was unhistorical and reactionary. Slavic nations, especially southern Slavs who needed the constant support of Russia, were also counterrevolutionary, without any historical meaning, and fated to disappear altogether. But they were far from alone. The Polish nation switched back and forth between the plus and minus columns. As a buffer between Russia and Europe, it was placed in the plus column, its historical mission to serve as a bulwark preventing a reactionary Russia from invading westward and impeding the forces of progress in Europe. However, when in the 1850s a wave of peasant revolts swept Russia, placing it on the Marxist train of history, Poland became an unhistorical nation, its nationalism regressive. Engel's tone changed.

> The more I think of the business, the clearer it becomes to me that the Poles as a nation are done for, and can only be made use of as an instrument until Russia itself is swept into the agrarian revolution. From that moment onwards Poland will have absolutely no more reason for existence. The Poles have never done anything in history except play at brave, quarrelsome stupidity. And one cannot point to a single instance in which Poland represented progress successfully, even if only in relation to Russia, or did anything at all of historic importance. Russia on the other hand is really progressive in relation to the East.

But when Russia overcame and suppressed the peasant revolts, and when Poland revolted against Russia in 1863, Engels and Marx became sympathetic to Poland once again.

My teacher's explanation that the regime's seemingly fickle attitudes toward nations were firmly anchored in Marxism was accurate. As was true of the original exponents of communism, the attitude of the Soviet regime's ideological guardians toward other nations depended on which were contributing to the advance of communism and which were not.

From Marx to Lenin, however, circumstances changed. Lenin lived in a different historical epoch. The Industrial Revolution was behind him. Russia had made a great step forward in its capitalist development, and the world revolution that Marx expected in the near future was a little late in coming. So Lenin declared that there was no need to wait for the whole world to become revolutionary. The proletarian revolution could happen in one specific country, Russia. Now the progressive movement toward the victory of communism demanded not the development of capitalist relations inside Russia but the overthrow of its regime.

Of course, this called for a new schematic of "good" and "bad" identities. Movements of national minorities inside the Russian empire were seen as progressive, since Lenin thought they helped weaken the Tsarist regime and increase the chances for the success of the revolution. In contrast, Russian nationalism, which served as the base of the Tsarist regime, was reactionary. Although nationalisms that weakened the Tsarist regime were considered good, they were only temporarily good. When the revolution comes these nations would melt away into the emerging communist paradise. As Lenin explained, our social-democratic party, the Communist Party, was the party of the proletariat; and its aim was to further the self-determination of the proletariat in each national group rather than the self-determination of the national group itself. A convoluted formula emerged that summed up communist attitudes toward nationalism: "we recognize the right of all these nations to self-determination, but we don't support their realization of this right."

To some, even this was too moderate. Rosa Luxembourg, a fiery Polish-Jewish Marxist, saw all forms of nationalism as reactionary; there was only one true motherland, the proletariat. Lenin took a more pragmatic position, insisting that nationalism in some circumstances could be used to promote the proletarian revolution.

It was Stalin—himself from a minority group—who at Lenin's request developed a theory of nationalism in a communist framework. In his work, "On the National Question," Stalin came up with the slogan that would accompany Soviet policy for decades: the Soviet Union would be "a culture national in form and socialist in substance." This would entail national independence, at least during the transitional period, before the world of differences would be replaced with a world of communist unity.

The theoretical period of Marxism-Leninism finished when the Bolsheviks came to power. Marx used to say that whereas before philosophers were explaining the world, his role was to change it. He believed that after the proletarian revolution, there would be no need for classes, religions, or nationalities. It was left to Lenin to prove his theory.

First he had to eliminate the classes of exploiters. Early Soviet identity cards listed people as proletariat, peasant, or bourgeois. Millions in the last two categories would be marked for destruction. All the property of the bourgeois, the rich peasantry, and the clergy had to be confiscated. In fact, the bourgeois itself had to be destroyed. As Michael Latsis, one of the leaders of *rasstrel*—which perpertrated mass executions by firing squad—explained in the newspaper aptly called *Red Terror*, on November 1, 1918:

> We are destroying the bourgeois as a class. Don't look during interrogations for materials and documents proving that the one who is accused was acting by word or deed against Soviet Russia. The first question which you have to ask him is: to what class does he belong? What is his origin, upbringing, education or profession? These questions have to define the fate of the accused. That is the essence of Red Terror.

In other words, they were to be destroyed not because of what they did but because of who they were.

Marx in the past had said that unlike the proletarian, who has nothing to lose but his chains and is therefore inherently revolutionary, peasants are connected to the earth and are therefore reactionary, slowing down the development of a classless society. Creating the brave new world necessitated destroying this rootedness. First the peasants' bread was confiscated, then their lands and farms, and finally their lives. The arrest and execution of the richer peasants started at the time of Lenin and was finished by Stalin in the beginning of the 1930s. Stalin's project of mass collectivization killed millions of people and turned scores of millions more into slaves of the state. The war against the peasantry was also accompanied by mass hunger, in which many more millions died.

Although there had been famine in Russia before, this time it became a tool to advance the revolution. The first

famine of the revolution, in 1920–1921, was used to undermine the strength and influence of the Church and to confiscate the only property that had not yet been taken. In a
secret letter to the members of the Politburo, Lenin made his
purposes crystal clear:

> Precisely now, when people are starving to the point of
> cannibalism, when on the roads you can see hundreds if
> not thousands of corpses, we can and we must organize
> the confiscation of all the church valuables, with the
> most unlimited and unmerciful energy. We must act
> without hesitation to destroy any resistance. The more
> representatives of the reactionary bourgeois and reac-
> tionary clergy that we kill, the better.

One would think that activists of the national movements were in a better situation than these condemned
classes. Stalin's formula of a culture "national in form and
socialist in substance" seemed to leave some room for
national life. But the interests of the revolution were para-
mount. At every cultural event, Soviet officials would censor
forms of expression that were not permissible. National languages and culture were judged based on whether they
deepened national prejudices or advanced the idea of a
future communist paradise. All other forms of expression
were the products of bourgeois nationalism, whose purveyors, if identified, would inevitably be faced with arrest,
exile, or execution.

Yet in this assault on national identity and especially
against Russian nationalism, which Lenin saw as the

strongest bulwark against revolution, there came an unexpected reprieve: the sudden attack of Hitler in 1941. Stalin's notional ally caught him totally by surprise.

In this bloody confrontation between two ruthless dictators, it became immediately clear to Stalin that communist slogans about class solidarity, the world proletariat, and international friendship were not inspiring enough to mobilize the citizens of the Soviet Union for an uncompromising struggle. It took no more than a few days before the communist rhetoric was replaced by old appeals to identity. *Faced with an existential crisis, the same regime that sought to destroy nation and faith now placed its hopes in an appeal to nation and faith.* It invoked the traditions of the Russian people and the images of the grand military leaders of old, even of the great Tsars of the Russian empire. All sorts of church groups and the national groups were mobilized, and official propaganda was steeped in national rhetoric. In 1944 the communist anthem calling for the rise of the universal proletariat, the *International,* was replaced in the Soviet Union by a new anthem that invoked "Great Russia that built for ever this unconquerable union of people." The notion of a brave new world without classes, it turned out, had no force to inspire the peoples of the Soviet Union to action. The idea of defending one's home, one's roots, and one's history prepared tens of millions for enormous sacrifice.

The war proved only a temporary respite in the assault on identity. Stalin continued the fight against nonhistorical, reactionary peoples, who stood in the way of progress. Virtually entire nations were uprooted from Crimea and the Caucuses—the places where they had lived for many centuries—moved to Siberia and Kazakhstan, and turned into prisoners and slaves.

In the final act of Stalin's struggle to create a new Soviet man—Homo Sovieticus as he called it—he focused his sights on Jewish nationalism. In anti-Semitic propaganda, Marxism is often attacked as a Jewish theory. To be sure, many Jews were among the theoreticians of Marxism and the practitioners of the October Revolution. Many were among the leaders of the struggle against Jewish nationalism, believing that it would impede the forces of progress. Most of these Jews would burn in the fires of the revolution, either in the revolution itself, as its heroes, or in the purges which followed, as its betrayers. Most were destroyed without realizing what a monster they had helped create. But the overwhelming majority of the millions of Jews in the lands that would come under Soviet control continued to reject Marxist theory and cling to a three-thousand-year-old identity.

There were many nations that Marx didn't like, that he considered unhistorical. But Marx, whose grandfather was a rabbi, had a special place in his heart for hatred of Jews. He called the Jews a chimerical nation, devoid of any reality, and claimed that the God of the Jews is money.

Stalin's view of the Jews was not very different. In "On the Question of Nationalism," Stalin explained in detail why the Jews were not a nation. How can they be a nation, he asked, when they are scattered everywhere, with nothing to bind them together except religious prejudices which will, of course, disappear? During the war, when all nationalisms were mobilized to fight against Hitler, Stalin did the same with the Jews. He created a special Soviet-Jewish antifascist committee. The most popular Jewish leaders were convened and sent abroad to mobilize resources from Jews in America in particular and from the West in general.

But after the war, Stalin quickly reverted. He was determined to terminate the unhealthy Western connections that had been established during the war. The establishment of the State of Israel only heightened his suspicions of the Jews. He initially supported the State of Israel's creation in the hope that it would help him jettison the British from the Middle East. But he soon changed his mind when Israel proved uninterested in supporting communist hegemony and, through its role in the revival of nationalism among Soviet Jews, was considered a threat to his regime. Not surprisingly, Israel changed virtually overnight from a "good" nation to a "bad" one.

Stalin's war against Jews had a number of stages. Not wanting to show his cards, Stalin first arranged to have the head of his wartime Jewish antifascist committee, Solomon Michoels, the renowned Yiddish actor and one of the most popular Jews in the West, "accidentally" killed in a car crash. Then, one after another, the members of the committee who had been sent abroad were arrested and disappeared. Yiddish actors, writers, and poets were then arrested and killed. Finally, leading doctors of Jewish origin were arrested and accused of plotting to poison Soviet leaders. A big campaign against cosmopolitans, which everyone knew meant Jews, was launched across the Soviet Union. Every day in the Soviet press, the anger of the Soviet peoples was stirred up against "Zionist cosmopolitans."

The denouement was set for Spring 1953. The plan was that after the doctors' trial, sentencing, and execution, there would be "spontaneous" attacks on Jews followed by requests to Stalin from Jewish intellectuals to save the Jewish people from the "justified anger of the Russian people." Letters were already prepared and signed. Stalin was to order the mass deportation of Jews from the big cities to Siberia and Kazakhstan, where barracks were already prepared to receive them.

But fate, as it has so many times before, would rescue the Jewish people once again. Stalin suddenly collapsed fatally on Purim, the very day that Jews have marked on their calendars for over two thousand years to celebrate their miraculous reprieve from a plot of annihilation hatched by Haman, a Persian viceroy who would be hanged on the gallows that he prepared for his Jewish enemies. The barracks remained empty, the doctors were released, and after the arrest of the KGB head, Beria, the Stalin cult of personality was formally renounced. Still, the Soviet effort to keep people assimilated and educated in the empty culture of "national in form and socialist in substance" continued.

In the end, however, those strong identities helped keep the spark of freedom alive. Courageous *individuals* like Andre Sakharov and Yuri Orlov, continuing the great tradition of the Russian intelligentsia, challenged the Soviet system and exposed its lies. But beyond the critical spark provided by individual dissidents, the force that enabled the flame of resistance to grow en masse and eventually engulf the Soviet empire was provided by the nations and faiths that refused to succumb to the Marxist assault on identity. After the founding of the Helsinki Watch group, the first to join were the Ukrainians, then the Lithuanians and Georgians. Next were the Catholics, Pentecostals, Crimean Tatars, and many others who came with demands for justice. As for the nation Marx had called a chimera, the nation Stalin thought had never acted together as one people, ironically it played a key role in bringing the communist regime to an end. It was the movement to free Soviet Jewry—a movement that united Jewish communities around the world in a common purpose—that delivered the decisive blow to the Soviet regime. After decades of unceasing struggle, this movement punctured a hole in the iron curtain. And as we dissidents always suspected, the smallest tear in the weak fabric that held together the Soviet empire caused it to unravel.

Stalin was therefore the ultimate chapter in the struggle launched by Marxism. Marx and Engels determined the fate of nations in their theories. Stalin tried to implement their theory in practice. Yet, as became clear during the death throes of the USSR, this effort to destroy identity was a great failure. Millions were killed in the hope of eradicating identity. But at the very first moment of opportunity, people rose up to reclaim their past and reassert their identities.

As I learned in the prison camps, those with the strongest identities were the least likely to succumb to tyranny. Those who retained a sense of the value of history, of tradition, of community, those who saw a purpose in life beyond life itself proved the ultimate bulwark against Soviet evil. It was precisely those who valued difference that united in a common purpose to defeat the mass murdering ideology that killed in the name of a utopian world without difference.

The Soviet Union fell apart, and at that moment all the nations returned to their place in history, becoming "historical" identities once again. But the Soviet Union was itself abandoned by history. As for the Soviet Union, it disappeared. One of history's greatest ironies is that the only unhistorical identity proved to be Homo Sovieticus. That was the real chimera.

THE HELPING HAND OF USEFUL IDIOTS

The history of the rise and fall of the communist utopia which cost the lives of tens of millions of innocents could probably have been much shorter if it had been isolated and shunned by the democratic world. But one after another, intellectual representatives in the West played the role of what Lenin famously called "useful idiots." Those in this category were guided by a plethora of reasons, from a fervent belief in the Soviet ideal of equality to exceedingly critical attitudes of their own societies to an overwhelming fear of war. But regardless of the motives behind their naïve sympathy for a cruel Soviet regime, the result was the same: As the Soviets were engaging in mass murder on an unprecedented scale, the useful idiots in the West were busy defending them.

Well after the Soviet Terror had claimed its first millions, the visionary science-fiction writer, H. G. Wells, wrote about

Stalin that "I have never met a man more candid, fair, and honest," and later used his keen insight to assert that "Stalin owes his position to the fact that no one is afraid of him and everybody trusts him." George Bernard Shaw was no better, instructing his readers during the time of Stalin's purges that "we cannot afford to give ourselves moral airs when our most enterprising neighbor, the Soviet Union, humanly and judiciously liquidates a handful of exploiters and speculators to make the world safe for honest men."

The height of useful idiocy was perhaps reached by Leon Feuchtwanger, a German-Jewish historian who fled Germany to France in the 1930s. Like many other liberals, he connected his antifascist hopes to the Soviet Union. Arriving in Moscow in 1937, the bloodiest year of Stalin's terrors, he told his readers that while everything is so pessimistic in the West, people were "teeming with optimism" in Russia. Knowing a first-rate dupe when he saw one, Stalin permitted Feuchtwanger to come to one of his famous show trials. Tired of torture and frightened by threats against their families, former leaders of the Soviet Union confessed regretfully at the trials to assisting foreign secret services and professed their undying devotion to the communist cause. One after another, they were sentenced to death. Feucthwanger's tunnel vision didn't disappoint the dictator. Reporting on the trials, Feuchtwanger informed Western readers how impressed he had been by the devotion of all sides to the communist ideal.

The American singer Paul Robeson was another frequent visitor to the Soviet Union. During one trip at the beginning of the 1950s, there were numerous rumors that Soviet Jewish poets, some of them personal friends of Robeson, had been arrested and had disappeared. He requested a meeting with one good friend, Soviet-Yiddish poet Itsik Fefer. The Soviet leaders were so certain of Robeson's sympathies that they permitted something they never had done before: They brought Fefer from prison to Robeson's hotel. Under the watchful eyes of the KGB, Fefer signaled to Robeson in gestures and half-sentences that he and his colleagues were under arrest and probably would be killed, entreating him to inform the world. But Robeson, like the many others who were blind to Soviet evil, did not fulfill this request. He continued to be a loyal supporter of communism all his life, and it was only as his own death approached—long after the death of Fefer—that he confessed to this story.

The phenomenon of useful idiots makes for more than a sad history lesson. By analyzing the reasons why so many people did not want to see, hear, or believe what was happening in the Soviet Union, and why so many responsible Western leaders kept speaking about shared dreams and aspirations between the free world and the Soviet Union, we can better appreciate why there is such a reluctance to confront today's totalitarians and the ideologies of hate that have bred them.

Marx once said that history repeats itself, first as tragedy then as farce. The tragedy finished, I found the farce in a small New York bookstore. In the beginning of 2005 I was speaking at university campuses. I had a few free hours and probably the same weakness as any author: wanting to see your book on the bookshelves. First I walked into a large bookstore that looked more like a department store. The salesman looked in the computer and told me that they had had a few copies but were sold out. I asked whether there was another bookshop nearby. He told me about a political bookshop around the corner. A few minutes later I walked into a small shop, piled with books and with gigantic posters plastering the walls. For a moment, I thought I had been transported back in time. Looking down at me were the faces of Mao Zedong, Che Guevera, and Ho Chi Minh. The books of Trotsky, Rosa Luxembourg, Lenin, and Stalin stared at me from the shelves. I was amazed. It was as if the battles of my past were jumping out at me. Then I saw the saleswoman, who perfectly captured the mood of the place. She was exactly like the commissars from the old Soviet films, with simple, severe, and merciless looks, wearing a worn-out leather jacket, drinking coffee, chain-smoking, and shouting into the telephone as if fighting for the revolution. Soon I realized she was shouting at someone from the warehouse who had not delivered her book orders.

Although I was the only one in the store, she was too busy with her revolution on the phone to pay any attention to me. She glanced at me with irritation as if I were interfering with her campaigns. I succeeded in slipping in one sentence: "Do you have Sharansky's book, *The Case for Democracy?*" She checked the computer, asked again what the name was, and then asked: "Why should we have this book?" "Because," I told her, "it is a political book and this is a political bookshop." Then she looked at me for the first time and said, startled, "Is it you who wrote this book? Are you Sharansky?" I said: "I am not asking about Sharansky but about the book."

Suddenly she noticed that people were standing behind me. "Who are these people?" she asked. "They are my bodyguards," I replied. "Leave immediately," she said in a raised voice. "I do not want gendarmes in my shop." "They will leave when I leave," I told her. "I am asking: do you have the book?" She came close to shouting: "We do not have your book!" "Thank you very much," I said. I left this shop which looked to me like a museum of natural history with strange creatures from the past. Classical Marxism-Leninism is dead; this bookshop is its grave. If only that had been the end of the assault on identity. But straight from this bookstore I went to the campuses of universities where I had to defend identity against a much more sophisticated attack.

THE ASSAULT OF POST-IDENTITY

The second great assault on identity after Marxism is late-twentieth-century post-identity theory. This theory comes in a variety of forms, from post-nationalism, which envisions a global society, to post-modernism, which sees each identity as unstable and all cultural forms as morally equivalent, to multiculturalism, which regards society as lacking any center but comprised of groups with equal claims and authority.

Post-identity inherits much of the Marxist vision, both of a world without meaningful difference and of identities that are labeled "good" or "bad" depending on whether they advance a particular goal. But there are also key differences. First and most obviously, whereas Marxism sought to strengthen the Marxist "identity" of class consciousness, post-identity works by weakening *all* identities, particularly one's own. Second, whereas Marxism fought for political power largely through Communist Party organization, post-identity has made culture its primary battlefield, conquering the universities and intellectual centers.

Post-identity theories are not as unified as Marxism. Marx had one clear answer to the problems of humanity, which was the classless society, as well as one clear path to achieve it, which was class struggle. These ideologies do not provide a single answer to the world's problems. But they share with Marxism the overriding dream of breaking down all barriers between people. According to the leading thinkers of post-identity, differences are seen as the cause of hatred, conflict, and war; nationalism and identity are the obstacles to worldwide peace and harmony. Therefore, these differences must be rejected in the name of creating a world of unity, equality, and justice.

Post-identity theorists see the devastation wrought by the wars of the twentieth century as a by-product first and foremost of nationalism and other forms of identity. Strong attachments or a sense of peoplehood, whether in ethnic, religious, or national terms, are regarded as fascistic and inherently aggressive. According to this view, these attachments led to war within Europe and colonial exploitation outside it in the name of a superior culture. The solution to war, conflict, and exploitation is therefore to transcend identity and nationhood and build a global society.

That post-identity thinking is an ideological response to war and conflict helps shed light on the moral vision that underpins it. While post-identity theories tend to be deeply relativist, all can agree on one absolute evil: war. Avoiding conflict is the ultimate goal and the ultimate good. After this is accepted and understood, the syllogism that drives the moral case against identity is perfectly compelling: *Identity causes war; war is evil; therefore, identity causes evil.*

To advance peace and justice, the root cause of evil—identity—must be addressed. This is a first principle of post-identity theories, from which flow many other post-identity ideas: from the notion that everyone should move beyond divisive attachments to become a "citizen of the world," to the dream of a United Nations, a European Union, and other supra-national forums that will suppress atavistic nationalism in the pursuit of this utopia, to the centrality of human rights in post-identity values.

In all forms of post-identity, as in Marxism, the ultimate vision remains a world without barriers, without identities separating people. As in Marxism, though all identities must be ultimately transcended, in the transitional period some identities contribute to this ultimate goal while some impede the final achievement of a world of harmony and peace. Therefore, as in Marxism, a division remains between "good" and "bad" identities.

Eric Hobsbawm, one of the founders and most prominent spokesmen of post-nationalism, draws the historical map exactly along these lines. Hobsbawm distinguishes between a "principle of nationality," which, transcending or combating narrow allegiances, he considers revolutionary, and "new nationalities," which he sees as "increasingly defined in ethnic-linguistic terms." The Hapsburg, Ottoman, and Russian empires transcended individual nationalisms. In a 1992 interview for *The Nation*, Hobsbawm stated that these empires "aimed to extend the scale of human, social, political, and cultural units, to unify and expand rather than to restrict and separate." The collapse of these empires, however, and the "unrealistic peace settlement" that was imposed by the leading powers after World War I, caused the emergence of the "new nationalisms" of separation and xenophobia, nationalisms that can be sustained, as he puts it, only by "mass exclusion, forcible assimilation, mass expulsion, or genocide." Third world anticolonial nationalists largely get a pass by Hobsbawm and remain "congenial," dismissing and subordinating "tribalism, communalism, or other sectional and regional identities as antinational."

Hobsbawm's division into progressive and reactionary nationalisms mirrors the Marx-Engels distinction. Indeed, the parallel is quite exact. Hobsbawm explicitly speaks about the reasons for the rise of new nationalisms unleashed by the collapse of the communist system, which succeeded in "imposing political stability over a large part of Europe" and whose downfall destroyed "the predictable planned economy and the social security that went with it."

It is important to remember that the Soviets imposed this "political stability" by sending its troops to Prague in 1948 and again in 1968, to Berlin in 1953, to Budapest in 1956, by building the Berlin wall, and by imposing an iron curtain on hundreds of millions. The "social security" was the security of the slave to get his food in the event he does what he is told.

Yet it is not surprising that the leading theoretician of post-nationalism would take a page out of Marxism. Hobsbawm joined the British Communist Party in the 1930s and was a longtime apologist for the Soviet Union, even justifying the Soviet intervention in Hungary when other communist historians refused to do so. In an autobiography published in 2002, long after the horrific crimes of the Soviet Union were exposed, this esteemed professor could still write that "to this day I notice myself treating the memory and tradition of the USSR with an indulgence and tenderness." For Hobsbawm, "The dream of the October Revolution is still there somewhere inside me."

Not all post-identity intellectuals dream of the October Revolution, but Hobsbawm's argument in favor of a world without nations remains widely influential and is echoed in the work of many others. For Mary Kaldor, a professor at the London School of Economics, there is a bad "new nationalism" that looks back, appeals to tradition, has deep cultural roots, and only serves to "legitimize existing states" through excluding "others of a different nationality." According to Kaldor, this nationalism is essentially violent, a "nodal point in the intimate relation between the modern state and war," and has in fact "much in common with religious fundamentalism;" that is, nationalism itself becomes a form of religious fundamentalism. Good nationalism—what she calls "small" nationalism—in contrast, is not cultural but political. Progressive, it accepts its own status as a temporary phenomenon aiming to play its part in the broader process of globalization.

Such "good nationalism" is in fact a form of cosmopolitanism—itself a core term for post-identity. Softened when presented as "rooted cosmopolitanism," it seems to make room for the differences of identity. Yet a recent president of the American Modern Language Association conveyed a similar idea in her presidential address: "Cosmopolites not only or even principally owe an allegiance to their place of birth but also to a broader, more worldly, supra and transnational worldview." Concrete identity, in contrast, remains tied to the "negative consequences of resurgent nationalism, ethnic separatism, and religious fundamentalism."

In the end, all these types of rooted cosmopolitanism, or "progressive" and acceptable nationalisms, come to one thing: The good nationalist is the one who is ready to give up his nationalism, the one for whom nationalism is unimportant. It reminds me of Stalin's formulation that culture must be "national in form and socialist in substance." You can enjoy nationalism as a kind of decoration, like going to a museum and appreciating all the different forms of art, or going to a festival and tasting the wide variety of ethnic foods. But real life, we are told, should be expressed not in these differences but rather in your obligations to humanity.

In the case of Marxism, this meant communism. In the case of post-identity, it is dedication to a world of human rights without conflict.

Post-identity has always been at the heart of the European Union. The preamble of the European Constitution proclaims that "while remaining proud in their own national identities and history, the peoples of Europe are determined to transcend their former divisions and unite ever more closely to forge a common identity." To post-nationalists, however, the European Union does not go far enough and is still too dependent upon nation-states. For Jurgen Habermas, one of the major political philosophers of the twentieth century, the goal instead should be "a federation whose common institutions take over state institutions," modeled on the United Nations Charter. Transnational government should go beyond "international law" as negotiated between states and "over the heads of the collective subjects" to give legal status to individual subjects as members in "the association of free and equal world citizens." Cosmopolitan organizations such as courts would guard against "processes of nationalist, ethnic, and religious fragmentation," towards a worldwide "common life without tensions among groups and peoples."

Post-nationalism appeals to a universal ideal, to a single global society. In this, it seems far removed from post-modernism, which generally rejects universals, pointing instead towards a relativism of cultural forms, none of which is ultimate or normative. Nevertheless, post-modernism became an ideological base of post-nationalism, and the reason is clear. If identities are accidental, as they are for post-modernists, they are unimportant in any meaningful sense.

In post-modern thought, national and other identities are seen as unnecessary fictions, even delusions. On the level of the individual person, the post-modern self is an unstable and constantly changing scene of social forces. Michel Foucault, working not surprisingly out of the Marxist tradition, famously describes the self as controlled and produced by institutions that "discipline and punish," institutions that are nothing more than exercises of power in competition with each other. If post-modernism sees individual identity as largely arbitrary, this is even truer of national identities. Nations are regarded by post-modernists as accidental and unstable aggregations of bids for power, a shifting kaleidoscope of fragments without intrinsic value that are continually rearranged, renegotiated, and recast. This is expressed in such notions as Benedict Anderson's "imagined communities" and Hobsbawm's descriptions of nations as "invented." Obviously, if nations are invented, there should be little difficulty in transcending them in the name of a global order not bound by national limitations.

Yet a third form of post-identity is multiculturalism. Born out of the mass immigration into Europe after World War II and the dissolution of European colonial empires, multiculturalism proposes dissolving national identity into whatever groups are present in a society, groups which often have strong transnational ties. A multiculturalist perspective declares the influx of immigrants into Europe as an opportunity for European societies to rid themselves of their preference for one culture and instead demand neutrality of the state towards whatever different cultures may arise. In fact, such multiculturalism denies special status to the culture to which new groups have come, including the democratic cultures on which multiculturalism itself depends.

Like post-modernism, multiculturalism is relativist. As Lord Bhikhu Parekh, one of the major ideologists of multiculturalism in Britain and chair of the 2000 report on "The Future of Multi-Ethnic Britain," puts it: "no culture represents the best life"; liberal society is "not the best, the most rational, or the only universally valid form of good society." Every culture has equal claims on public life. Lord Parekh rejects the idea of "selective immigration" as "a strange way to show international solidarity." According to this view, it is unacceptable for a state to establish criteria for citizenship in the name of preserving a given national culture. The ideal society instead is a mixed one, a conglomeration of groups rather than a nationally defined state.

Like post-nationalism, multiculturalism inevitably paves the way toward a globalized society. Thus, for example, in *Rethinking Multiculturalism,* Parekh proposes that the "traditionally close ties between territory, sovereignty, and culture" should be loosened and replaced by a "composite collective culture" that "nurtures diversity" and ultimately points beyond itself to a cosmopolitanism emphasizing "the interests of humankind at large." Tariq Modood, another prominent multicultural theorist, envisions a "new Europe" of "ethnic heterogeneity inserted into a multicultural superstate."

While placing few demands on the foreign cultures that have recently arrived in large numbers in Europe, multiculturalism is not equally tolerant of the previously dominant national cultures of Europe. Along with other post-identity ideologies, multiculturalism calls on European societies to weaken their own national uniqueness and recognize that European cultural tradition should not be defining and determinative. In effect, these ideologies deny the right of a national culture to sustain itself and, by refusing to make value judgments about cultural forms, call into question the supremacy of the very democratic culture that has enabled different groups to coexist in mutual respect or tolerance. As these post-identity ideologies have systematically hollowed out Europe's unique national identities and cultural forms in the name of peace, equality, and justice, groups without democratic experience or traditions have flooded into Europe. And these groups do not have the slightest qualms about the supremacy of *their* identities.

A DEFENSELESS EUROPE

The inevitable confrontation between the post-modern West and modern fundamentalism has been perceptively described in numerous books: Melanie Phillips's *Londonistan,* Ayaan Hirsi Ali's *Infidel,* Bawer's *While Europe Slept,* and many others sound the warnings. They describe how in mosques in the center of Europe, imams openly spew the most extreme language. Despite being funded by the very governments they denounce, they vilify Western life as decadent and Western democracy as infidel and false. Today, in communities in European cities, gender apartheid is entrenched, genital mutilation is practiced, forced marriages are commonplace, severe restrictions are imposed on women's movement and education, and women are murdered in honor killings. As Sevran Ates, a Berlin lawyer of Turkish origin who works with women trying to escape forced marriages, puts it: "There are two societies with two different value systems living side by side, but wholly apart, in Europe." Although statistics of honor killings are not kept in Europe, Britain has begun reexamining two thousand deaths and murders between 1996 and 2006 and has so far reclassified over one hundred homicides as honor killings.

Above all, there is the threat of Islamic terror in Europe, from the Madrid and London bombings to the murder of Van Gogh to the death threats against the likes of Salmon Rushdie, Ayaan Hirsi Ali, and Magdi Allam, an Egyptian-Italian writer who has been targeted because of his criticism of terrorism and his defense of Israel's right to exist. Public safety has become an urgent question, with repeated warning of further terrorist attacks. The director-general of Britain's MI5, for example, has warned that thirty "Priority 1" terror plots are currently under investigation, with two hundred terrorist networks involving at least sixteen hundred people, many of them connected to Al Qaeda leaders in Pakistan. Thousands of Britons are reported to be training in militant camps in Pakistan, intending to then return to Britain.

One would hope that in the face of this menacing threat, European societies under attack would be able to mobilize Europe's citizenry to defend the democratic culture that they spent countless centuries building and endured unimaginable sacrifice preserving. But the triumph of post-identity ideology among the intellectual classes in Europe and its permeation into mainstream discourse has made this seem all but impossible. Faced with this threat, the culture that Europe seems most concerned with defending is a politically correct world anchored in post-identity. Thus, with the acute threat facing Britain by Islamic extremism, Prime Minister Gordon Brown banned his ministers from using the word *Muslim* in connection with security and refers not to *terror* but to *criminal acts*.

Why should Europe agree to disown its own cultural norms? Why should it dissolve its national cultures and unravel its bonds to both past and future in the name of other cultures or global citizenship? Why does Europe not rigorously oppose this nondemocratic community within its midst?

Here we must return to the logic of post-identity: *Identity causes war; war is evil; therefore, identity causes evil.* Although it may seem obvious that the answer to Europe's problems lies in vigorously defending the identity that is under assault, we must remember that to many Europeans, identity is a *cause* of evil.

The problem is compounded by the deep feelings of guilt that Europeans feel towards many of these groups. The European past has many episodes of injustice and exploitation. Because of its prior crimes, European countries are seen by many to have a historic responsibility to open their doors to those they formerly oppressed and be tolerant of their cultural traditions. There is a hesitation to judge others and a sense that those who suffered in the past must be largely excused from current obligations or norms. As Parekh writes, "the experiences of colonial oppression and totalitarian domination," the experience of being "oppressed and humiliated culturally," has created the "need for cultural rights."

Here again the world divides into "good" and "bad" identities. The identities of the oppressed remain good because they deserve compensation for the injustices of the past and are opposing those who perpetrated those injustices. No less important, the expression of those good identities helps weaken the identities of the guilty and oppressive Europeans who should not defend their tainted histories and traditions.

Guilt, then, is the first powerful force serving to neutralize Europe's response to the fanaticism in its midst. Fear is the second. Democracies, which place great value on human life, are very vulnerable to fear. This vulnerability becomes acute for a democratic society that has a weakened sense of identity. Like prisoners with a weak identity who are concerned only with their personal safety, leaders pay any price to avoid bloodshed; everything will be sacrificed in the name of keeping the peace.

The combination of guilt and fear inevitably leads straight toward appeasement. This was true in the 1930s when guilt over the harshness of the Versailles Treaty toward a humiliated Germany and the fear of a rising Nazi power combined to paralyze the democratic world. How much more debilitating is that paralysis today when after decades of post-ideology theories permeating the culture, the West lacks a firm belief in its own values and identity? Indeed, it is difficult for a society that has been waging war on its own identity in the name of peace to reverse course and now rebuild what they have been systematically trying to dismantle for two generations.

CHAPTER 4

Post-Identity and the Collapse of Human Rights

WHY HASN'T THE POST-IDENTITY commitment to human rights shielded Europe from an intolerant fundamentalism? The answer lies in a warning Eleanor Roosevelt, one of the authors of the Declaration of Human Rights, issued in September 1948. In those years, the Soviet Union was working tirelessly to sow moral confusion in every international forum:

> We must not be deluded by the efforts of the forces of reaction to prostitute the great words of our free tradition and thereby to confuse the struggle. Democracy, freedom, human rights have come to have a definite meaning to the people of the world which we must not

allow any nation to so change that they are made synonymous with suppression and dictatorship.

Today human rights has become a tool primarily to vilify those societies that hold it most sacred while largely ignoring the regimes whose entire rule is predicated on the wholesale abandonment of a culture of human rights.

In this new Orwellian world, the arsonist and firefighter are deemed morally equivalent. The outrage that greets the news of civilian casualties who are victims deliberately targeted by the terrorist is matched by the outrage that accompanies the news of civilian casualties who are the tragic but unintentional consequence of legitimate acts of self-defense. How did this happen? How did the concept of human rights become twisted beyond all recognition so that it can be employed both as a weapon assaulting its greatest champions and as a shield protecting its greatest abusers?

After World War II, the leaders of the battle-scarred democracies were determined to create a world without conflict. In this spirit, they established the United Nations, which would succeed where the League of Nations had failed: to help secure international peace and stability. Central to this struggle was a commitment to defend the rights of the individual. At first it looked as though the lessons of World War II had been learned: Namely, that you can't accept and trust leaders who deny the rights of their own people, and that respect for other peoples begins with respect for your own citizens. Appeasing regimes that do not value the lives and liberties of their subjects is a formula for war and aggression.

The advance of liberal democracy, it was thought by many, was the best guarantor of a stable and peaceful world. It was no accident, therefore, that the first central international document drafted in the wake of the war was the 1948 Declaration of Human Rights. This was not a declaration in favor of a particular ideology or a preference for a particular way of life but rather a call for making human rights a foundation of the new international order.

Totalitarian regimes immediately and correctly perceived themselves threatened. The Soviet Union, and its numerous satellites, fought inside the UN to shift the focus of human rights from political rights to economic rights, so that the declaration spoke less about the freedom of citizens from state control and more about the obligation of the state to provide loyal citizens with work. According to the Soviets, it was up to the state, of course, to define which citizens were loyal.

Although Western countries agreed to make some compromises and the final text included both political and economic rights, the Soviet Union still viewed the documents dangerous enough that even thirty years after these rights had been declared you could not obtain a copy of the UN Declaration of Human Rights in a Soviet library or bookshop. They were available only through underground *samizdat* publications, which were confiscated in every search by the KGB along with other "subversive" literature. The Soviet fears were justified: An international document that mandates the protection of citizens from arbitrary state power is a serious challenge to any totalitarian regime.

The attempted check on tyranny was undermined from the start not merely by the Soviets' geopolitical position as a Security Council superpower but by post-identity ideologies that were already beginning to take root in the West. For example, in a statement accompanying a special amendment to the Declaration of Human Rights prepared by the American Anthropological Society, the AAS explained the "problem" that the declaration was failing to resolve:

> The problem faced by the Commission on Human Rights of the United Nations in preparing its Declaration of the Rights of Man must be approached from two points of view. The first, in terms of which the Declaration is ordinarily conceived, concerns the respect for the personality of the individual as such and his right to its fullest development as a member of society. In a world order, however, respect for cultures of differing human groups is *equally* important (emphasis added).

Labeling the focus on individual rights a Western European and an American idea, the AAS argued for a broader declaration that would recognize that "standards and values are relative to the culture from which they derive" and that there was "no technique of qualitatively evaluating cultures."

> Ideas of right and wrong, good and evil, are found in all societies, though they differ in their expression among different peoples. What is held to be a human right in

one society may be regarded as antisocial by another people, or by the same people in a different period in their history. The saint of one epoch would at a later time be confined as a man not fitted to cope with reality.

At first glance, this cultural and moral relativism seems idealistic. All cultures are regarded as equal. There are no high and low races, no good and bad peoples, no good and bad cultures or societies. But in practice, it means that no human rights' standards can be universally applied, no values transcend time and space, no principles are sacrosanct. Alan Bloom was one of the first people to warn of the dangers of a valueless society. In his *Closing of the American Mind*, he writes about how he would challenge his students who all assumed they were moral relativists by asking what they would do as a British viceroy in India if a religious community there wanted to follow their timeworn tradition of burning the wife of a deceased husband along with him. The common answer provided by the students—that the British shouldn't be there in the first place—didn't really resolve the issue.

The principal problem with this relativistic approach is actually much simpler. The AAS, like so many other organizations who claim to be concerned with human rights, makes a seamless transition from cultural relativism to *regime relativism*. That is, the "political regulation of group life" established in a particular country is seen as an expression of a country's underlying culture.

Perhaps this argument may have some merit when comparing, say, Britain's parliamentary system with America's presidential system and the unique histories that determined their respective development over time. But it is not true that the difference between democracy and tyranny is simply a matter of culture. North Korea and South Korea are born of the same culture. One is a totalitarian state, the other a free country. East and West Germany shared a culture and history but the political system in each country was different. So West Germans were free and East Germans were not.

Anticipating the obvious problem that existed even in 1947 of having to reconcile their cultural relativism with individual rights, the AAS nevertheless found an answer that only reinforced their belief in the former:

> Even where political systems exist that deny citizens that right of participation in their government, or seek to conquer weaker peoples, underlying cultural values may be called on to bring the peoples of such states to a realization of the consequences of the acts of their governments, and thus enforce a brake upon discrimination and conquest. For the political system of a people is only a small part of their total culture.

Every time I reread this passage I am astonished at its recklessness. These words no doubt will give little consolation to the many millions who have been wrongfully killed, tortured, and imprisoned since 1948, nor will they offer much comfort to their families. Anyone who has lived under a tyrannical regime knows that the "political system" lays claim to the "total culture." That's why one of the synonyms of tyranny is totalitarianism.

An attitude of cultural and moral equivalency is one of the axioms of post-identity, and the relativism it engenders is the main reason for the moral blindness of the movement for human rights. As cultural relativism spills into regime relativism, governments that trample wholesale on basic rights that people who live in free societies take for granted are held on the same moral plane as democracies. It becomes enough to declare, "Our culture doesn't share the values of the West and its forms of democracy," and immediately the sacred principle of the equality of cultures turns back any demands for rights from the free world. Such demands are classified as impermissible interference into home affairs.

During the Cold War, the Soviet Union used this argument many times, and an entire generation of Western politicians was ready to accept it. Regime relativism was a handy cover for a desire to avoid conflict at any price, for the temptations of appeasement, and for a genuine fear of the Soviet Union. The final collapse of the Soviet Union owed nothing to the moral relativists but everything to the courageous struggle of dissidents and the bold leadership of a few leaders in the West who possessed enough moral clarity to see those dissidents as their true allies. The readiness of different dissident groups and movements to fight, to risk their lives and freedom, to appeal to the moral sense and common sense of the free world, is what ultimately proved that the Soviet Union and the West did not hold values that were morally or politically or culturally equal.

But it wasn't easy. Dissidents and activists in the Soviet Union and in other communist countries had to take huge risks to ensure that the Soviets could not hide behind the curtain of moral equivalence that post-identity thinkers offered and to ensure that the West's professed commitment to human rights would become more than lip service. The decision to create a group to monitor the Helsinki Accords of 1976 was made out of concern that the West would permit the Soviet Union to turn this important agreement, which placed the USSR's human rights record on the international agenda, into another exercise of empty words. At the time, I proposed to organize a kind of discussion among independent representatives of international public opinion to debate whether the provisions of the Helsinki Accords were being fulfilled.

But Professor Yuri Orlov, a thoughtful and courageous Russian dissident, did not agree with me. We will not destroy the wall of indifference by discussions, he said. We have to declare the creation of a group and start collecting and publishing information about specific violations of this agreement by the Soviet Union. We will be arrested. But then it will be impossible to avoid discussion of these problems internationally. He was right. In one year, all the founding members of the Helsinki Watch group were arrested or exiled. I was accused of high treason. But the question about the Soviet Union's human rights record and demands that it should abide by the Helsinki Accords accompanied the Soviet Union until it ceased to exist fifteen years later.

PEACE AND HUMAN RIGHTS

In today's world of activism, two different impulses have now come together: the demand for human rights and the peace movement. Both movements were born after 1945, when the United Nations, the pan-European movement, and post-identity ideologies in general emerged in reaction to World War II, determined to prevent anything like it from happening again. Although sister movements, the two remained in certain senses distinct, at least up until the end of the Cold War. Until then, the human rights movement was partially saved from moral equivalence because of the fate and treatment of the dissidents behind the iron curtain, which many genuine human rights advocates chose not to ignore.

But from the outset, the peace movement was a weapon in the hands of the Soviet Union. The desire to live without threats and aggression and the distrust that so many feel towards politicians who they believe use war to advance their own political ambitions are feelings that unite tens of thousands and even millions of people in the free world. It is so obvious to them that all people want peace to the same extent and in the same way. That is why ideological debates in the struggle for peace are brushed aside. The answer to peace activists is as clear as day: Everyone should unite against war and for a better world.

In this atmosphere it is difficult to understand—and there is a strong motivation against understanding—the vast difference in the attitude of dictatorial regimes and democracies towards peace. It was difficult to accept that a constant state of aggression, of a brinkmanship that left the country constantly mobilized for war, was essential for the Soviet regime's survival, as is true for all totalitarian regimes. The rulers must keep their own people under constant control. To do this demands a threat from both inside and out—a threat that is used to justify their own harsh measures and to further extend their own power.

So the Soviet Union used the peace movement immediately after the war, not for peace but as part of its own campaign against the West. It created its own Committee for the Defense of Peace. The Committee's purpose was to cultivate friendly "direct connections between the activists for peace in the West and Soviet citizens." Mutual conferences, festivals, demonstrations, and marches were designed to support the high spirit of this international solidarity. People from the Soviet Union were permitted to participate in these staged activities, or more exactly, they were mobilized to participate in them. The degree of involvement depended on the extent to which the regime trusted the participant.

One of my acquaintances in Moscow was a pensioner, an elderly lady who had decided to study French and wanted to have a pen-pal. The only safe way to correspond with anyone abroad was to propose your services to the Committee for Peace. She was assigned a nice idealistic French couple who were active participants in the peace movement. Before writing every letter, she was given detailed instruction from the Committee as to what she should write and how she should answer questions posed to her. The letters were sent through the Committee, which, as she explained, was better because their censorship was lighter than the general censorship applied to every letter sent abroad. After some time her young French pen-pals wanted to visit Moscow to see their elderly friend. But the Committee proposed she wait. First she had to prove her loyalty. Although she was a good citizen, she was still Jewish and therefore a liability. Only after years of working through this Committee, with her actions dictated by them, with her letters used to impart official messages—only after years of correspondence that looked like a friendly, personal exchange but was actually an official exchange—was she permitted to invite the French couple to Moscow. Before official approval came for her to participate in international conferences, she died.

In the beginning of the 1980s, peace activists in Europe poured into the streets of Germany, England, and other countries. They passionately demanded the removal of American missiles from Europe. Marching alongside them were Soviet "peace activists" who also demanded that America remove its military bases from Europe. At that time, the real Soviet peace activists—those who were demanding the removal of Soviet bases from Europe—were languishing in prison with me. The fate of these people was somehow not the concern of the peace activists in the West.

In contrast to the peace movement, human rights activists could not simply ignore the fate of dissidents in Poland, Czechoslovakia, and the Soviet Union. Amnesty International dutifully published information about prisoners of conscience in the Soviet Union; some of my friends were imprisoned merely for sending this information to them. Human Rights Watch in New York—its earlier name was Helsinki Watch—was created in response to the Helsinki Watch groups in the Soviet Union. These organizations made the violation of human rights in the communist world the focus of their work. Europeans could make faces when Reagan called the Soviet Union an evil empire. They could accuse America of being overly aggressive in its plan for strategic missile defense, derisively referred to as Star Wars. But even those who were critical could not fail to see the evil of the communist regime that was sending troops to Czechoslovakia, arresting the leaders of Poland's Solidarity movement, and keeping hundreds of thousands of Jews and other nationals behind the iron curtain against their will.

The final victory of the West in the Cold War was achieved because human rights became a central focus of international relations. But this was both the start and the end of what proved to be one short episode of moral clarity. Exactly as in 1945, the downfall of the Soviet Union brought for a brief period the impression that the forces of evil had been destroyed and that the world was now secure. Now what remained, it was thought, was to remove the root of future conflicts, to end the scourge of nationalism.

But as the champions of post-identity had taught, some nationalisms were worse than others. There was the bad nationalism of a strong West and the good nationalism of a weaker third world. The latter's nationalism was permissible because of the injustices done to them, because they were fighting to right past wrongs. Even if they did not act exactly according to our own value system and rules, they could be understood. After all, theirs is a justified nationalism directed towards removing injustice. Thus, moral clarity gave way to moral relativism.

The refusal to recognize the profound difference between democratic and non-democratic regimes undermined the moral clarity of leading human rights organizations. When Amnesty International published its reports on the violations of human rights, it never distinguished between the countries that recognized human rights and those that did not.

As a result, the volume of human rights violations they report is often a function of the transparency of the country they are reporting on. The more open the country, the more free the press, the more outspoken the opposition, the greater the potential that violations will be exposed. There is nothing wrong in this as long as the difference between open and closed societies is understood.

Unfortunately, Amnesty International still will not create separate categories for democratic, authoritarian, and totalitarian countries. They refuse to "label" states, yet the need to do so is obvious: The worst year of human rights abuses in a democratic America would not equal a single day of abuse in a totalitarian North Korea.

The hypocrisy and double standards of the international human rights organizations reflect the disappearance of clear moral criteria that alone can guard human rights. A refusal to see the difference between free and totalitarian societies, between a state at peace and a state at war against terrorist regimes, undermines the universal values on which a claim to human rights is based.

A commitment to human rights is above all a commitment to democracy and freedom and to the right to defend them. To equate all cultures, to refuse to distinguish between those that are democratic and those that are not, is the profoundest betrayal of human rights. Only a combination of a robust defense of democratic life and a rigorous denunciation of abuses can uphold and defend human rights. It is acceptable to hold democracies up to a higher standard as long as you recognize that democracies, by definition, are already maintaining higher standards.

In its refusal to distinguish democratic from nondemocratic regimes, the human rights movement undercuts its own commitment to democratic freedoms and itself becomes a tool of undemocratic powers. The principle of human rights has not succeeded in its role as the guardian of Western democracy because, in the end, this guard and guarantor of Western values is blind: It can no longer recognize the critical moral distinction between democracy and totalitarianism.

Grievance Resolution or Ideological Struggle?

In the battle of ideas, totalitarian, antidemocratic forces should be on the opposite side of post-identity ideologies. These two are diametrically opposed in their value systems, their aims, and their methods. One is in violent confrontation with the world of democracy and freedom. The other, which has made human rights a core value, is an inseparable part of the democratic world. But this clear opposition in principle breaks down in practice.

True, dictators treat the world of freedom and democracy with hostility, fear, and disdain, as one should consider an ideological enemy that endangers your very existence. But post-identity ideologies treat the totalitarian world with understanding. According to these theories, specific grievances, not ideology or ideas, have brought societies, countries, groups, or individuals to such an "unnatural" state of hatred and violence. The goal becomes clarifying and removing the underlying reasons for hostility—essentially redressing grievances. So instead of confronting root causes grounded in ideology and profound, consequential differences between opposing world views, battalions of conflict-resolution groups (which are, in effect, grievance-resolution groups) are popping up everywhere.

Focusing on grievances rather than ideology creates a basis for cooperation between two forces that should be inherently inimical to each other: a post-identity human rights community and fundamentalist totalitarian groups with no interest whatsoever in human rights. More exactly, it gives totalitarian forces an opportunity to use the ideology of post-identity to avoid condemnation and pressure, and to have a free hand in advancing the regime's interests.

When grievance becomes the focus, groups such as Al Qaeda can win sympathy by grounding their hostility in the latest "atrocity" committed by the West. When Al Qaeda's battle against us is seen as an ideological struggle of radical Islam against the West that has been waged in different forms for centuries, then grievances such as the stationing of troops on Saudi soil, the situation in Iraq, or cartoons depicting Muhammed take on a different meaning. They are correctly seen as pretexts for the assault rather than as a root cause of the assault. But when grievances become the main focus, the pretext is confused with the cause.

Certainly there are real grievances, and if there is inequality, if there is poverty, if there is injustice, it should be addressed. Moreover, ignoring grievances can exacerbate an underlying ideological conflict. But treating grievances will not solve or address ideological conflict. It is like trying to deal with the smoke but not the fire.

We see this confusion between grievances and ideology in the terrible battles of the twentieth century. In general, democracies see war as their very last option. It is therefore tempting to try to avoid direct conflict by addressing the grievances of the other side instead of confronting their ideas. This was a preferred and popular approach long before post-identity prevailed in the West, and Nazi Germany is the most familiar example. The leading politicians of England and France hoped that in recognizing the legitimate grievances of the German people, they could satisfy Hitler. Rather than confront an aggressive, hate-filled Nazi ideology or challenge a brazen regime that was building its military muscle and destroying all those principles that democratic nations cherished, they made one concession after another. But appeasement only made things worse. The growing power of Nazism and the fear it aroused seemed only to strengthen further the desire of Western politicians to appease the Germans in order, as they fooled themselves into thinking, to remove the reasons for a possible war.

Likewise, the communist idea of the dictatorship of the proletariat was never in itself popular in the free world. But the idea that much of the world's problems were due to economic exploitation and injustice, and that the Communists fighting for the classless society were therefore on the right side of history and progress, was popular among intellectuals in the free world. So instead of struggling against the aggressive communist ideology, which was eliminating and annihilating whole classes and peoples, Western liberals concentrated their efforts on dialogue and trade cooperation with the USSR. They thought if they stopped their own cruel capitalist exploitation and their oppression of the poor and the weak, this would bring them into harmony with the Communists. But this type of approach gave communist regimes the opportunity, in the name of class struggle, to repress and destroy populations, confiscate property, and spread their ideology further and further across the world. And in this they were aided by the voluntary assistance of hundreds of thousands, if not millions, of activists for peace, cooperation, and mutual understanding.

For the post-identity mindset, it is even easier to look for explanations not in ideology but in grievances because the belief in absolute values is rejected and the idea of Western guilt plays a central role. In the confrontation between Muslim fundamentalism and the free world, the idea that terrorist acts are the result of grievances connected to economic, political, and other injustices is widely shared. Grievances are to blame and not the ideology of Wahabbism, which teaches hatred towards Western civilization and is cultivated by the religious centers in Saudi Arabia and has moved from there to Europe, Asia, Africa, and America. Downplayed as well is the brainwashing by extremist sects of Khomeini and his followers, which calls for and predicts the victory of Islam over the infidels and guarantees a place in paradise to every *shahid* who goes forth to destroy the infidel enemy. What is blamed instead is poverty and inequality in the third world, created and amplified by the policies of transnational monopolists, by the Israeli occupation of Palestine, or by American aggression in Iraq. Crimes of the West are seen by many as the reason for hate speeches against Western civilization in the mosques of London and the riots of desperate youth in Paris.

The grievance-resolution approach blocks understanding and prevents appreciating the danger of ideologies that create, support, and direct terrorist attacks. The conflict is about fundamental differences in outlook. Calling these differences "grievances" is mainly a way of avoiding facing them or, even worse, giving up on what you believe and giving in to beliefs that directly oppose yours out of fear of confrontation.

Replacing the demands of ideological struggle with grievance-resolution can happen without anyone even noticing it. Tony Blair was one of the few politicians in Europe who seemed to recognize the reality of ideological confrontation. In a television interview right before he left office, he courageously addressed British Muslims: "Nobody is oppressing you. Your sense of grievance isn't justified," and added: "The reason we are finding it hard to win this battle [against terror] is that we're not actually fighting it properly. We're not actually standing up to these people and saying, 'It's not your methods that are wrong; your ideas are.'" But soon after finishing his term as prime minister, in his new office as special representative of the Quartet in the Mideast, he retreated to the grievance-oriented position that not Arab dictatorship, not Islamist fundamentalism, but the Israeli-Palestinian conflict is the true problem of the entire region. Conflicts that are rooted in a struggle of ideas are covered over as conflicts that seem local or economic or to involve specific claims of territory that only need to be met to solve the problem.

This approach not only fails to solve the real conflict but helps perpetuate it. It fails to deal with ideology and the methods for teaching and spreading it. It doesn't address the war of ideas that is being waged—the outpourings of hate propaganda against America and the West, the anti-Semitism widespread throughout the Muslim world, the brainwashing for suicide-terrorism, the destruction of democratic initiatives throughout the Arab world. For it seems easier to deal with the grievances and to press for their removal than to confront the ideological motives, the ideological methods, and the ideological ends that are the true basis of the hatred.

NOTHING TO DIE FOR

The world of post-identity is especially ripe for the grievance-resolution approach for another reason. For even when moral distinctions have been recognized, when evil is called by its name, many lack the strength to fight it. And they lack the strength for a simple reason: because identity has been under assault for three generations.

The effort to weaken identity has taken a profound toll on many aspects of democratic life, and the struggle to advance human rights is no exception. If there is no real distinction between places that recognize human rights and those that do not, there is no sense or justification to risk your life to defend one way of life over another. Somebody living in a hotel, suddenly finding it uncomfortable, will not protest and struggle to change the conditions. He will move to another hotel. Author Oscar Van den Boogaard, asked why Europe did not resist the attacks by fundamentalists, said in self-mockery: "I am not a warrior, but who is? I have never learned to fight for my freedom. I was only good at enjoying it."

If individuals are not bound by a commitment to history and tradition, if the connection between generations is broken and destroyed, there will be no passion and depth of emotion. If all identity is seen as fluid, if nationality is merely political and not cultural, if it is seen as imaginary and therefore deluded, the mystic connections in time and space—what Abraham Lincoln called the mystic cords of memory—are lost.

In prison, I learned that without a commitment beyond yourself, the fear of death will inevitably control you. What is true for an individual is true for a society. Without a strong identity, without a commitment to a particular way of life, without a feeling of connection to the generations who came before and to those who will come after, there can be enjoyment of life but not the strength to defend that life when it is endangered. In fact, a negative side effect of the good life available in democratic societies is that it can often weaken the very strength to fight for it. It may lead to a willingness to pay any price in an attempt to rescue and safeguard a life not connected to anything beyond the self. But this insatiable desire for the safety of the self can become the greatest danger to the safety of all, including ourselves.

The exponents of post-identity who used World War II to propel their project to rid the world of strong identities in the name of peace were wrong. *What prevented peace then was not the presence of strong identities but the absence of democracy. What was needed in the wake of the war was not a weakening of identity but a strengthening of democracy.* The same is true today.

In failing to focus on strengthening democracy, the purveyors of post-identity create a moral muddle that undermines the struggle for human rights. And in undermining identity and embracing relativism, they weaken the ability of democracy to ward off aggression. Unlike tyrants, who force men to the front on pain of death, democracies must rally the will of a free people to defend themselves against aggression. What provides that will if not a strong identity? One must value a culture to defend it, and one must love a country to be willing to make the ultimate sacrifice for it.

People are willing to make sacrifices when the choice is clear, when they know what is right and what is wrong. Yet if nothing is right, if no value judgments can be made, then nothing is wrong. Post-identity has created a world in which there is no right. But if there is no right, why fight? In such a world, the enemies of democracy have a great advantage. *They* are prepared to fight and die for their twisted beliefs. Identity is the only force that will give us the strength to resist and ultimately to defeat them.

CHAPTER 5

Identity in the Public Space

IN 2003, I WAS INVITED to participate in a conference in Paris on anti-Semitism organized by UNESCO. Politicians and public figures—among them Nicholas Sarkozy, then France's interior minister—said that it was absolutely unacceptable for France, in terms of its history, principles, and record, to tolerate the explosion of hatred against Jews and the campaigns of demonization against both Jews and Israel that were then occurring. At the time, a wave of attacks saw synagogues burned, cemeteries desecrated, and Jews harassed in the streets. It became so dangerous that the chief rabbi of Paris recommended that observant Jewish men not wear *kippot*, the traditional head covering, in public.

But the passionate speeches only proved what was obvious to everybody: Both Jews and Israel were under assault in France. Muslim extremists and leftist-liberal intellectuals, despite their ideological differences and despite employing very different arguments, joined in massive protests against Israel. Tellingly, at a rally protesting the Iraq war, anti-Semitism trumped anti-war solidarity when members of a left-wing Jewish organization were beaten by Muslims marching alongside them.

While attending the conference, I thought it would be a good idea to meet with French-Jewish intellectuals involved in human rights issues. I wanted to hear their reaction to the rhetorical assault that was being made in the name of human rights against Israel, the sole democratic country in the Middle East. Moreover, I wanted to hear their response to the argument voiced in some quarters of France's Jewish community that the actions of the Israeli government were encouraging anti-Semitism.

A meeting was quickly organized by a hospitable couple, well-known among Jewish-Parisian intellectuals. What I heard at that meeting stunned me. To be sure, everyone agreed that the excesses of Muslim religious fanatics were unacceptable. But I shouldn't forget, the intellectuals told me, that the fanaticism was happening against the background of the failure of Zionism. Even if Zionism had once been a good idea—a point that apparently not everyone was prepared to concede—that point was in the past. "East is East and West is West," they said. "You can't bring the West to the East and expect it to work." This reminded me of Alan Bloom's experience when he challenged his students' moral relativism. In both cases the students and the intellectuals preferred not to be in locations where their democratic beliefs were challenged. Nonetheless, they were confident that France was not anti-Semitic. "You will see this when the Zionist experiment is over and the Jews have to leave Israel. Then we in France will do our best to attract the biggest share of Jews back as citizens."

"You are part of us," they told me, "part of Europe, part of European culture; and we need you for the real battle of the future."

"And what," I asked curiously, "was the real battle?"

"The real battle is not some marginal skirmish against Muslim fanatics," they answered. "The real battle is over how our world will look, over what our culture will be, over the shape and direction of the free world. The battle is not between Islam and the West. It is between civilized Europe and the United States."

To hear America described as the enemy of Europe would have surprised me at any time. But two years after 9/11, at a moment of such clear and urgent confrontation between the free world and the world of totalitarianism, when Europe itself was facing a challenge from radical Islam both inside and outside its borders, this attitude toward the country that had fought with France in two world wars and which had helped secure Western Europe for over half a century was absolutely astounding.

Hatred towards America is ubiquitous in Europe today. An essay in *Foreign Affairs* spoke of "a growing divergence between America's perception of its moral leadership and European perceptions of the United States as a flawed super-power."

But those who place most of the blame for such divergence on the foreign policies of the Bush administration are mistaken. The essay was published in May 2001, barely three months after Bush became president, and well before 9/11 altered the course of American foreign policy. The seeds of anti-Americanism were planted long before the former Texas governor strutted into the Oval Office. In his 1989 account of *America*, French post-modernist Jean Baudrillard, wrote, "America is a world completely rotten with wealth, power, senility, indifference, Puritanism and mental hygiene, poverty and waste, technological futility, and aimless violence." Since the end of the Cold War, European complaints against America have been wide-ranging, from American capitalism to Americans' support for capital punishment to the spreading influence of American culture in an age of globalization. It was in 1999 that French Foreign Minister Hubert Vedrine warned that France "cannot accept a politically unipolar world, nor a culturally uniform world, nor the unilateralism of a single hyperpower." He might as well have said that France could not accept America.

Only nine months after 9/11 and nine months *before* American troops were sent to Iraq, an essay in a June 2002 issue of *Newsweek* examined the "new transatlantic bad feeling" and concluded that there was "a serious clash. But is this new and rising, or something particularly attributable to George Bush? Not at all."

For many critics in Europe, Bush is a caricatured but still representative illustration of what is widely regarded as a crude, simplistic, naïve, and moralistic American society.

The same criticism was made of Ronald Reagan's famous "Evil Empire" speech, which was described by Andrew Alexander, a British conservative columnist for the *Daily Mail*, as an "oversimplified view of the world." Former Prime Minister James Callaghan agreed, confident that "the Europeans have a better understanding of the complexities of the present world difficulties than the United States." Former French Foreign Minister Couve de Murville similarly dismissed American foreign policy as failing to take "realities into account." And Robert Kaiser, writing in the *International Herald Tribune*, commended a conservative British editor who described the Reaganites as having "alarmingly simplistic beliefs that divide the world into goodies and baddies."

News of this speech reached me in prison and was for us political prisoners a ray of hope in the darkness of the punishment cell. We not only recognized the truth of Reagan's moral distinctions—how could a regime that murdered, massacred, exiled, and imprisoned innocent people *not* be evil?—but also knew that to resist the evil empire and to defeat it you had to call it for what it was and deny moral relativism.

History vindicated Reagan, not his sophisticated critics. But today we can hear again and again opinions such as those of Dominique Moïsi, a special adviser at the French Institute for International Relations, who recently argued that "the combination of religion and nationalism in America is frightening. We feel betrayed by God and by nationalism, which is why we are building the European Union as a barrier to religious warfare." Many Europeans looking at America see an insane materialism on the one hand and a boorish, religiously inspired, Manichean division of the world on the other. Conversely, many Americans see Europeans as cowardly, self-indulgent, dependent on American protection but ungrateful for it, and willing to appease any aggressor that threatens their comfortable way of life.

To be sure, these generalizations have significant exceptions. The peoples who live in countries once under Soviet influence have notably different attitudes toward America— attitudes that undoubtedly have been shaped by their first-hand experience. And even in the heart of "Old Europe" there are exceptions, foremost among them being Sarkozy. The new president of France has unabashedly reaffirmed French ties to America, noting that France "owed" to America the "fact that we are free people and not slaves." The French president even went so far as to say that America "had built the greatest nation in the world."

Still, the predominant attitude toward America in Europe is negative. Noting the deep hostility to America in French political discourse, Jean Francois Revel trenchantly observed in *La Grand Parade* that "if you remove anti-Americanism nothing remains of French political thought today, either on the Left or on the Right."

IDENTITY IN EUROPE AND AMERICA

Part of this hostility can be attributed to the very different concepts of identity and democracy that lie at the core of the American and European world views. The latter stakes everything on cosmopolitanism, a universal ideal in which barriers between people fall and all cultures are valued equally within the framework of a global society. How these various cultures are to be sustained without commitment, without cultivation, when diversity becomes at most a rooted cosmopolitanism, is something not accounted for. In this model, what is important is that peace and democratic rights transcend difference.

The American perspective sees a world in which diversity is embraced, with various individuals and groups committed to specific histories, traditions, and ways of life. But each one is linked to the other through a common commitment to democracy. Not only is the protection of the right of everyone to express their particular identity highly valued but participation in collective democratic life is itself a powerful source of identity. Democracy is valued as a means and an end.

In America, particular identities co-exist alongside one another, sometimes overlapping or intercrossing and sometimes distinct from each other. But the social framework does not require that differences be smoothed away. It requires only commitment to a system that protects the rights of everyone and values the common public life that sustains that system. In this model, democracy and identity do not oppose each other, but support and strengthen one another.

Europe's history has been one in which identity and democracy have been largely at odds with one another.

There has been a tendency to define identity as an exclusive and unitary tie to place, tradition, and customs, and to define democracy as exactly transcending and erasing these ties. The choice presented in this struggle is seen as clear: One can embrace the particular or the universal; be a citizen of a nation-state or a citizen of the world; be a member of a particular faith devoted to his co-religionists or a humanist devoted to all mankind. In short, one can embrace identity or democracy but not both. Given this pervasive view, it is no surprise that in today's Europe, identity and democracy glare at each other from different sides of the barricade.

The Fault Line of the Veil

Europe faces a monumental challenge from Muslims who are not integrating into broad European society. For many, the veil has become the most visible manifestation of this failure. But the veil is also an integral part of the identity of many Muslims. Like a fault line where two different land masses come together to create an unstable and dangerous crack between them, the veil is a dividing line not simply between different cultures but between identity and democracy.

In 1989, three girls were expelled from a French school for refusing to take off their headscarves in the classroom. The controversy about wearing the veil has been restaged again and again in different European countries concerning different forms of covering. In France it eventually led to a 2004 law banning the wearing of headscarves and other "conspicuous" religious symbols in public schools, among them the *kippah* and a visible cross.

The argument in favor of the ban was straightforward. The veil is seen as a sign of difference. Wearing it distinguishes an individual as belonging to a distinct group. The French authorities do not wish to see such differences intrude into what they believe should be a neutral public space. The law was broadly supported, with public opinion polls indicating that about seventy percent of the French were in favor of the measure. Even among French Muslims, forty-nine percent of women favored the ban and just forty-three percent opposed it. There was a fear that if the headscarf were allowed, those who did not wear it would face pressure, even harassment, to do so. Permitting the veil, it was thought, would lead to coercion, putting individual choice and liberty at risk. Those opposed to the veil championed the principle of a neutral public space, a place that could help nurture a common life from which religious differences are excluded. Proponents of this view argue that abiding by this principle is the best way to strengthen a democratic society.

But is this really true? If wearing a veil is an integral part of a woman's identity, if she sees it as an expression of her commitment to her faith, does forbidding her from wearing it make her more loyal to European society or less so? Is forbidding the veil really the way to balance the demands of identity with the protection of democracy?

I have my own experience with head coverings. After my wife, Avital, arrived in Israel in 1974, she began to become more religious. A great deal of her strength came from her faith. Sometime before my arrest she decided to don a head covering—a religious tradition for Jewish married women (unmarried girls do not cover their hair, although all religious men do). She wrote to me about the decision, explaining that it strengthened her connection to me and to the sources of tradition that had become so important to her.

But she was concerned that the head covering would seem to me too drastic a change; she thought that she was perhaps moving too far too fast into a different religious world. She wrote that if I were opposed to it, she would remove her head covering. I respected her feelings, but at that time the head covering meant moving very quickly in an unknown direction, and who knew where that would lead? So I replied that I preferred that she remove it. For some time she did. But about a year after my imprisonment, while Avital was traveling and fighting day and night all over the world for my release and to free Soviet Jewry, she decided to put it back on. Under the new circumstances of my imprisonment, it was much harder to correspond with me, but she succeeded in sending a note through my mother. In it she explained that it was very difficult for her to be divided between her faith and her actions. She needed to express outwardly her inner life and inner beliefs. As a dissident who had broken out of the world of doublethink and was strengthened by my own inner freedom, I recognized the power of what she was saying. It was clear to me that if the head covering was important to her, if it helped sustain her, then she *should* wear it. The head covering had become a reflection of her innermost self, a part of her identity.

In the summer of 2007, former dissident and president of Czechoslovakia Vaclav Havel, former president of Spain Jose Maria Aznar, and I organized a conference on security and democracy in Prague. It became a forum for democratic dissidents from all over the world: from China, Russia, Belorussia, Sudan, Cuba, and also from all over the Middle East—Lebanon, Egypt, Saudi Arabia, Syria, Iran, and Iraq. Among the two hundred participants and guests, two women wore head coverings: my wife and Zainab al-Suwaij, the head of the American Islamic Congress. They became friendly, and Zainab gave my wife a present, a nice Arab *kisui rosh*—head covering—with a note attached: "To my sister in faith." And I was thinking all the time: How would she feel if her daughters were not permitted to go to an American school (she lives in Washington, D.C.) wearing a headscarf?

European countries have responded to the question of the veil in different ways. Most agree that if the covering conflicts with professional performance, it should not be permitted. Britain banned the *niqab* (full-face veil) in school as inappropriate to the role of a teacher. But the discomfort extends beyond practical considerations. Prime Minister Tony Blair called the veil "a mark of separation." In Germany four states have banned teachers from wearing headscarves. Various towns in Belgium have banned the *niqab*. The Dutch government has imposed a total ban on the wearing of *burqas* and other Muslim face veils in public "in view of public order (and) the security and protection of fellow citizens." This is the first European countrywide ban on Islamic face coverings. But there is a wide perception of the veil as a barrier. And indeed, the veil can be a barrier when imposed on women as part of a wider and systematic practice of restriction.

Once I was speaking to a European group of politicians who were sympathetic to my positions on the link between democracy and security and would therefore, by European standards, be considered conservative. The subject of the veil came up in our discussion. Given our general agreement on most of the important issues of the day, they were shocked that I opposed the French law and that I supported the right to wear a veil in public (barring professional reasons for preventing it). If you permit the veil to some women, they argued, it will make it more difficult for girls and women to resist the pressure from their families and communities to wear one and as a result integration will be much more difficult, particularly for women.

I responded with a question: Is your concern that more people will wear the veil or that they will do it under pressure? Both, they answered. That is the problem, I explained. Of course violent pressure in the family—beginning with the veil but extending to all sorts of restrictions on women, from not being able to leave the house and not having access to education to physical abuse to honor killings in the most extreme cases—must, like all acts of inequality and violence, be resisted by each society with all its power. That is a democratic obligation. But you see a problem even when people freely choose to wear a veil. Identity itself is problematic for you. You want to protect democracy by banning identity. It looks like an easier way to combat extremism, I told them, but it's wrong and the price for such actions will be very high.

The French law banning the veil means that the French believe that dramatic expressions of identity weaken and threaten their society. It means that they believe that preserving democracy necessitates the shedding of strong identities and the establishment of a purely neutral public space that is unmarked by sharp cultural differences. Only then can conflict be avoided and equality protected. Freedom, according to this view, does not include the freedom to be significantly different, the freedom to choose to identify deeply with some particular culture or history or religion. In short, to protect freedom of choice and to uphold democracy, it is necessary to give up identity; the more there is of one, the less there is of the other.

What this ultimately leads to is a kind of public hypocrisy, not neutrality. French Muslims are coerced to act one way while thinking and feeling another. To insist that people hide their identity, that they never present or express it in public, does not strengthen democracy. Just as Avital felt a kind of contradiction between her inner beliefs and her external behavior when she took off her head covering, so anyone who wishes to express their religion in their dress will feel frustrated and unnatural when denied the right to do so. This frustration creates resentment against the law and alienation from the society that passed it.

Expressions of religious identity have very different meanings in different contexts. To some women, the veil is not only a religious obligation but a manifestation of their own culture and an expression of who they are. To deny them the right to wear it becomes a form of repression. A law banning the veil, far from strengthening a sense of participation in democracy, can only cause hostility to it.

Instead, what the state should fight unequivocally is not the expression of identity but *the rejection of democracy*. This is true of the veil or of any other specific cultural custom. Pressure, harassment, and violence, like other undemocratic acts or restrictions, need to be forcefully opposed: by legislation, education, and intervention when necessary. Society must make a clear statement that an absolute principle of democratic society is a norm of nonaggression, where one cannot forcibly impose one's views on others. New citizens must accept this norm. When there are irreconcilable conflicts between customs and democratic norms, customs must give way, whether that means vigorously prosecuting honor killings and genital mutilations or banning underage marriage. But nothing is intrinsically undemocratic about wearing a veil.

Instead of defending democratic norms, post-identity Europe undermines them. Citizenship has been granted without requiring language skills, civic education, or even conformity to laws against polygamy. Mosques and schools receive state funds despite anti-Western agitation and indoctrination. European countries have pursued many different strategies, from multiculturalism to assimilation to exclusion, but the record shows disintegration rather than integration. In France there have been widespread and recurrent riots, with policemen afraid to enter certain areas and a tremendous increase in anti-Semitic incidents. In Britain, opinion polls show that almost twenty-five percent of British Muslims think the 7/7 bombings can be justified because of the war on terror. Nearly half think 9/11 was a conspiracy between the United States and Israel.

But Britain is not the only country in Europe facing this problem. Annual estimates indicate that tens of thousands of European-born Muslim women are forced, often with the threat of death, into unwanted marriages. Overall estimates for genital mutilation in Europe put 22,000 girls at risk, with 279,500 already affected. In the UK there are an estimated 3,000 to 4,000 new cases each year.

Yet there is reluctance to discuss or record these forms of violence for fear of being called racist and being vilified for creating an atmosphere of discrimination. In the most absurd, downright Orwellian example of this, terrorism perpetrated by Muslims in the name of Islam has been defined by British Home Secretary Jacqui Smith as "anti-Islamic." Ayaan Hirsi Ali's repeated attempts as a member of the Dutch Parliament to establish a database identifying honor killings and the national origins of those who commit them were repeatedly opposed on the grounds of being discriminatory. Her calls to document genital mutilation by requiring medical examinations and reports were rejected as illiberal. When at last she initiated her own investigation to determine how large the phenomenon of honor killings was, she discovered that in the period between October 2004 and May 2005 alone, there were eleven honor killings in just one of twenty-five regions of the Netherlands.

Political correctness, cultural relativism, and multiculturalist ideologies that proclaim that any cultural practice has the same moral validity as any other make it much more difficult to challenge the propagation of extreme forms of Islamic fundamentalism. At the same time, oppressive laws banning the harmless wearing of veils make fundamentalism more likely.

The French decision to ban the veil in schools coupled with the enormous tolerance toward the coercion and repression that daily transpires in many Muslim areas within that country is instructive. Rather than confronting coercion everywhere at all times, thereby establishing a clear norm of nonaggression, the French authorities have decided instead to make what they regard as a principled stand against the wearing of the veil. The result is that many see in the authorities' opposition to the veil not an application of a sacred principle of zero tolerance for coercion that is cherished by democracies but rather an assault on an expression of identity that threatens no one.

Democracy does not demand the sacrifice of identity, nor does democracy inevitably lead to a universal cosmopolitanism devoid of real meaning. On the contrary, as America has shown for two centuries, democracy is reinforced by strong identities and a universal ideal can be enriched by a deep sense of attachment to one's people, culture, and nation.

America's Shared Public Space

In America the story of the veil has a different ending. When in 2004 an American school in Muskogee, Oklahoma, tried to forbid an eleven-year-old Muslim girl from wearing a headscarf, the state interfered not on behalf of the school but on behalf of the girl. The state not only failed to see the need to restrict the girl; it defended her right to express her identity. Similarly, in response to the French ban that same year, a resolution was introduced by the top Democrat on the Human Rights Subcommittee, sharply criticizing the government of France for restricting the free expression of religion. It passed overwhelmingly.

So why is the veil not seen as a problem in America? The difference is one of attitude to public space in general. America is often described as maintaining a neutral public space. But in practice it is better to say that public space in the United States is not neutral but shared, in accordance with certain democratic norms. Any place outside a private home, private building, or private institution is public. The state cannot demand that anyone abide by a specific identity nor can the state discriminate in favor of a specific identity. Whereas in France expressions of identity in such public spaces are seen as a threat to democracy, in America expressions of identity are seen as acts that are protected by the norms of democratic life and further strengthen those norms. In America everyone is free to bring their identity into the public space. While the French champion an *identity-less uniformity,* America celebrates an *identity-rich diversity.*

A close Jewish friend of mine from America once worked for the late Democratic Senator Henry Scoop Jackson. He wanted to show his boss how dedicated he was, so he came to Capitol Hill on a Jewish holiday. Senator Jackson asked him: "Why are you here? Isn't this your holiday?" My friend answered: "The work for you is more important." Senator Jackson, who was not Jewish himself, responded: "Look, my boy, if you really want to be a good American you should be a good Jew." Thus, in the most public of public spaces, the American Congress, one finds an attitude not only of toleration of identity but of respect and even encouragement for its various expressions.

What seems entirely natural to many Americans is almost unheard of in Europe. In the early 1990s, I visited Oxford University, a bastion of academic freedom, where I met with one of the most independent and powerful philosophical minds of Europe, a man for whom I felt friendship, great respect, and admiration. I mentioned how impressed I was by the activity on campus of the representatives of Chabad, a Jewish outreach group dedicated to bringing Jews back to their tradition. He vehemently disagreed: It was, he said, a dangerous and provocative activity. "We Jews should never forget that we are guests here. Our Jewishness should be kept for our homes and for our families. It should not be part of our public life."

The differences in the American and European outlooks toward identity are deeply rooted. It can be seen in the history and values of the American Revolution as compared to the French. The United States was born out of American religious tradition and identity no less than out of political traditions of democracy and Enlightenment. The early town meetings were held in the same meeting houses that also served as churches. The procedures of voting, debate, and discussion that elected magistrates were based on those for electing ministers. The sense of individual conscience, answerable to and acting within community, originated in a Protestant religious sensibility that became the basis for congregations and then for political participation. And from the start, partly by default and partly by design, America was born a diverse nation and has remained a diverse nation. It is true that the Europeans came to America intending to claim it for themselves, disregarding native populations who they ultimately displaced. But the European settlers were themselves diverse, coming from different religious groups and different countries of origin, no one of which could control the others. Besides the English settlers on the Atlantic Coast, the Spanish settled Florida, the French settled Canada and New Orleans, and the Germans, the Midwest. Religious life was no less varied. There were German Protestants and Puritan Calvinists in the North, Anglicans in the South, Catholics in the Mid-Atlantic, Quakers in Pennsylvania, Dutch Reformed in New York, and many dissenters all over the place. Beginning with Roger Williams, the founder of Rhode Island, a colony devoted to religious freedom, theologies soon developed that held freedom of conscience to be a religious right and considered its preservation a religious duty.

Forged out of this diversity was a sacred shared value and, ultimately, a common identity, best expressed in the motto chosen for the seal of the fledgling nation—*E pluribus unum*: Out of many, one. America has always been an immigrant society and not an ethnically unified one. Yet the founders vehemently rejected the ideas that today underpin multiculturalism. They refused requests to establish states according to language or ethnic or religious type. And they designed a common civic education that would train all Americans in the skills of literacy and debate necessary for self-government and, no less important, that would join them in common memories, histories, and devotions. These policies were not designed to forbid or repress individual expression according to religious, ethnic, or other affiliations. Pluralism, not multiculturalism, was the American model (the great and awful exception to this pluralism being race, where blacks endured slavery for nearly a century after America's birth and de jure segregation for another century).

Increasingly through the nineteenth century, staggering influxes of new populations arrived, not only from Protestant Northern Europe but from Catholic Europe (Ireland and Italy) and from Catholic, Greek Orthodox, and Jewish Eastern Europe. These masses adopted an American identity in addition to their ethnic ones, what has been called American hyphenation: Irish-American, Italian-American, Polish-American, Jewish-American, Asian-American, and, although with much greater strain and after centuries of persecution, African-American identities.

In such hyphenated—or what we might call linked—identities, the hyphen is a "plus" not a "minus," as Michael Walzer, one of the leading writers on identity, democracy, and pluralism, memorably put it. Or in the words of another leading specialist in American immigration, John Higham, hyphenation builds both ethnic and American identity. Moreover, American identity is itself a genuine identity, not merely an empty vessel. It includes what has been called America's civil religion: civic participation in memory and history, marked through shared events on the calendar, shared principles and ideals, and shared hopes and aspirations. At the heart of this identity remains a commitment to democracy itself. When Americans were asked in a 1958 survey on "Civic Culture" just what made them Americans, their overwhelming answer was "freedom." But freedom also has a history, and devotion to freedom is an identity, which is strongly manifested in a firm commitment to a society where one is free to express one's own identity and where others are extended that same freedom.

In my experience, Americans tend to have a stronger, more assertive, less embarrassed national identity than contemporary Europeans. Integration into American life is not painless or seamless. But the American ideology has traditionally been one of diversity linked through a common civic life.

While the American Revolution drew upon religious practices and sensibilities, the French Revolution was based on their rejection. American clergy were among the most vocal supporters of the Revolutionary effort, but the French Catholic establishment was seen as the core enemy of French Republican aims and its ethos. Intimately tied to the oppressive structures of monarchy and the land-owning and governing elite, the church was viewed as a yoke whose overthrow came to define French liberty. America never had a nationally established church, and the period after the Revolution saw the disestablishment of churches from the colonial period, which in any case witnessed an enormous multiplication of different denominations, each voluntary, self-organized, and self-supporting. The clause in the Bill of Rights guaranteeing freedom of worship and forbidding the establishment of religion keeps American religion voluntary. But this has not weakened it. On the contrary, it has strengthened it. In fact, freedom itself is seen as a sacred religious principle. As America's Declaration of Independence famously puts it, man is endowed by his *Creator* with certain inalienable rights. Even Thomas Jefferson, author of the Bill of Rights and whom secularists praise for establishing the wall of separation between church and state, couched the rights he so fiercely championed in specifically religious terms: "Almighty God hath created the mind free, and manifested his Supreme will that free it shall remain, by making it altogether insusceptible of restraint." In his classic work *Democracy in America,* published in the 1830s, Alexis de Tocqueville noted that America offers an "intimate union of the spirit of religion with the spirit of liberty."

This intimate union is lost on many Europeans, who tend to see American individualism as atomistic, lacking in community, and expressed above all in materialism and cultural emptiness. At first glance, the European critique of American materialism is in many ways a powerful one. The incessant drive for self-advancement, the feverish pursuit of self-interest, and the worship of success and wealth can be atomizing and emptying factors in American life. But American individualism is not restricted to materialism alone. It is also the basis of an unmatched spirit of voluntarism and of a civic culture that allows so many ways to express solidarity with others who share values and goals. Paradoxically, American individualism may in no small measure be responsible for the continued and recurrent turn to religious community in America. It is a way to restore connection to others, where actions extend beyond the self, where you break out of the prison of self-interest into a wider sense of contribution to purposes larger than your own.

The American experience shows that religious participation, like other forms of identity, is not antagonistic to democracy. Democracy instead is the guarantor of its expression and exercise. Expressing religious and other identities becomes itself a sign of democracy, not a threat to it. Religious life flourishes precisely because it is a mode of personal expression as well as community solidarity. The French Revolutionary idea, which in the name of liberty, equality, and fraternity emphasizes the ideal of *sameness* of all citizens, tends to regard religion—as it does all other strong identities—as divisive. The French Revolutionary government established departments that purposely cut across regional cultures to incorporate them into a uniform state, run from Paris. Dialects were forbidden. Speaking anything but standard Parisian French was outlawed in schools long before headscarves were.

But the American Revolutionary idea of freedom took a different view of the role played by diversity in democratic life. As James Madison wrote in the Federalist Papers, article 10:

> Liberty is to faction what air is to fire, an aliment without which it instantly expires. But it could not be more foolish to abolish liberty, which is essential to political life, because it nourishes faction, than it would be to wish the annihilation of air, which is essential to animal life, because it imparts to fire its destructive agency.

To America's founders, faction was a natural by-product of democratic life and, in an important sense, also its guarantor. The multiplicity of interests, along with the system of checks and balances built into the U.S. Constitution, ensured that no one group would dominate others. Here, a multiplicity of strong identities and the multiplicity of views that flow from those divergent identities become critical to the preservation of democracy.

THE CASE OF AMERICAN JEWRY

For myself, the most familiar case of diversity of identity and its expression—or lack thereof—is of course the Jewish one. Here, the contrast between Europe and America is stark. European nation-states have a long tradition of intolerance and exclusion by a ruling and majority identity. Thus, democracy came to be defined in opposition to identity altogether. In fact, it was out of this opposition that the notion of a neutral public space was born. Napoleon

defined emancipation as the release from particular identities. Put simply, liberty meant equality, and the price of it
was renouncing difference.

In pre-Enlightenment Europe, things would have been
difficult for any minority. But for Jews, vilified for well over
a millennium as the embodiment of evil, this was especially
true. For most Europeans, Jews were not merely the conti-
nent's ubiquitous "other," the sizeable minority population
in their midst; they were widely seen as betraying all basic
principles of decency and morality. Shakespeare had quite
possibly never met a Jew since they had been banned from
England for nearly three hundred years before his birth.
Nevertheless, he created his infamous Shylock with the
stereotypes that had shaped—and partly because of his *Mer-
chant of Venice* would continue to shape—the image of
Jews for centuries.

The history of Jews in Europe before the Emancipation
was one of rejection of difference through discrimination,
persecution, and expulsions, which included expulsions from
England in 1290, from France first in 1182 and then finally
in 1394, from Spain in 1492, and from Portugal in 1497. In
the provinces of Germany where Jews were permitted resi-
dence, their right to remain was always under review, keeping them under constant expectation of expulsion, restricted
in their professions, and forbidden from owning property.

When the winds of Emancipation began to blow through
Europe, Jews were presented with a choice. They could
become equal citizens but only by keeping their Jewish identity restricted to private life. Many Jews, understandably

eager to break free of generations of persecution, embraced the offer. Judaism was reformed to meet the demands of this civic invisibility, with the German Reform movement leading the way. By instituting a number of significant changes, from translating the Hebrew liturgy into German to celebrating the Jewish Sabbath on Sunday rather than Saturday to abolishing traditional dietary restrictions, Reform leaders hoped to help the Jews become full partners in German life, to be what one Enlightenment thinker would later call "a Jew at home and a man in the street." Significantly, the German Reform movement did not see Jews as a separate nation but rather considered themselves to be "Germans of Mosaic persuasion."

But the Enlightenment strategy of fading out of view was deeply and tragically unsuccessful. Enlightenment and emancipation promised to treat Jews as equal citizens provided they remained invisible as Jews. But what started with eliminating Jewishness from the public square culminated in an attempt to eliminate Jews altogether. The country where Reform was born would also be the country that would condemn the Jews to extermination.

Europe's democratic ideals would leave no room for Jewish identity. On this point, there was little that separated the philosophical ends of ideologies associated with the Right or the Left. Each had a dream of *sameness* and *unity*, whether it entailed a fascistic single identity or imagined the dissolution of all identity. In a sort of inverted mirror but one with a deep inner logic, Nazi totalitarianism echoes utopian universalism. They each reflect the heritage of European culture in which democracy and identity oppose each other, in which there is no room for substantial difference. Put simply, identity in Europe had to be uniform, either by insisting that everyone had the same identity or that everyone had no identity. In either of those worlds, Jewish identity had no place.

The first Jews who came to America brought with them attitudes forged in Europe. Coming mostly from Germany until the great waves of flight from the pogroms of Eastern Europe and Russia of the 1880s, the early Jewish movements were typically Reform. These Jews insisted, as they had in the Old Country, that Jews shared a religion and not a nationality. In 1885 a conference of Reform leaders declared: "We consider ourselves no longer a nation, but a religious community," with the Bible nothing more than an expression of "the moral and philosophical progress of respective ages."

Yet as these European Jews became Americanized, they become *more* willing to express their separate Jewish identity. A closer inspection of the evolution of the platform of Reform Judaism in America is striking on this point. By 1937, the same Reform movement that had a few years before not considered the Jews a nation was now declaring that "Judaism is the soul of which Israel is the body," and that in Palestine "we behold the promise of renewed life for many of our brethren." They felt obliged to help build a Jewish homeland. In 1976, after four more decades of Americanization, the same Reform movement that once saw itself as a bridge toward assimilation began to show a critical distance from the surrounding culture rather than merely a thirst to melt into it: "The widespread threats to freedom and the spiritual emptiness of much of Western culture has taught us to be less dependent on the values of our society and to reassert what remains perennially valid in Judaism's teaching." As for Israel, Reform declared itself "bound to that land and to the newly reborn State of Israel." By 1997, Reform Judaism was affirming "our ancient covenant and our unique history among the nations to be witnesses to God's presence."

In Reform Judaism, as in other denominations, there has been a steady move away from the fear of maintaining a separate identity to a sense that it is precisely only such an identity that can be sustained over time. This willingness to assert difference, coupled with a deep sense of American identity that leaves ample room for this assertion, is powerful evidence of how America's democratic life accommodates and facilitates the expression and exercise of identity.

The idea of Jewish identity as a legitimate part of an American identity, as part of a loyal citizenship, played a major role in the building of the powerful movement in America that struggled to free Soviet Jews. The solidarity of Jews with their brethren behind the iron curtain was expressed in many countries but nowhere else was this effort connected in such a powerful way with a country's own core values. Nowhere were Jews ready so openly to connect the struggle for Soviet Jews with advancing the basic interests and values of the state. In struggling on behalf of Soviet Jewry, American Jews were expressing *both* of their identities simultaneously. As Americans, they were championing the rights that democratic societies take for granted and that the Soviets were denying their subjects: freedom of speech, religion, assembly, and of course, freedom of immigration. As Jews, they were standing in solidarity with their people.

Joining the struggle to free Soviet Jewry became as American to them as marching in the civil rights movement, as American as protesting against apartheid in South Africa, as American as calling for an end to genocide in Sudan.

America's Jews did not shy away from the struggle because they were Jews. They embraced it. Almost every synagogue and every cultural and community center was turned into a battlefield. The battle then moved to the Congress, the Senate, the White House, into the heart of government. It was a twenty-five-year struggle that involved hundreds of thousands of people.

In helping to rescue Soviet Jewry, the American Jews also strengthened themselves. There is a saying in Hebrew: More than the Jews keep the Sabbath, the Sabbath keeps the Jews. In fighting for the rights of Soviet Jews, American Jews gained a new sense of themselves. After my release from prison, I traveled throughout America and had the opportunity to thank American Jews for their support. In meeting after meeting, I heard the same message. "It is we who have to thank Soviet Jews. You have given meaning to our life and to our Judaism." A neighbor in Jerusalem, an immigrant from New York, who was watching me play with my young daughters, shared a similar sentiment when she said to me with a nostalgic sigh: "You know, Natan, it was such a great time when you were in prison: the energy, the passion, the activism, the meetings." I nearly apologized for having been freed.

The final act of that twenty-five-year struggle came in the massive rally in Washington, D.C., timed for President Mikhail Gorbachev's first visit to the United States on December 7, 1987. It was a time of great hopes for a rapprochement with the Soviets. Some of the Jewish organizational leadership was nervous: Might such an open challenge to the Soviet leader at a time of improving relations be seen as warmongering?

I disagreed, convinced that this was the historic moment to finally break open the gates of the Soviet Union for all who wished to leave. After being told by the experts that only a few thousand Jews would brave the cold to come to Washington in December, I moved with Avital and our baby daughter Rachel to the United States four months before Gorbachev's visit and went to more than thirty cities to mobilize support for the rally.

Grassroots American Jewry, comfortable with their own identities and passionate about the struggle for Soviet Jewry, did not share the anxieties of some of the organized leadership. They came in droves: By car, by bus, and by plane, over 250,000 American Jews descended on Washington, proudly demanding of Mr. Gorbachev: "Let my people go."

Any concerns that the rally would be seen as un-American quickly evaporated. Jewish congressmen told me the next day that it had been a great moment for them, that their colleagues had come to congratulate them for the example they gave to all Americans on how to defend their principles.

Identity and democracy were not at war. They were on the same side, reinforcing one another in a struggle against a regime that denied both. And the power of their union proved decisive. Using democratic means in the name of democratic values, the defense of identity received enormous sympathy. When Gorbachev asked Ronald Reagan to abandon his demands for freedom of immigration, Reagan, referring to the mass demonstration taking place on the mall, said: The American people won't let me.

American eyes do not see identity as a threat to public life, as long as it is expressed voluntarily and not coerced by government. When done freely, expressions of identity generally win public support. For example, in 2006, when a town council in Fort Collins, Colorado, voted to prevent the placing of a menorah in the town square, residents—mostly non-Jewish—protested by lighting menorahs in their homes, and a local pub made its courtyard on the square available for a public menorah.

Needless to say, Jews are not the only case of diverse identity in America. American immigration tends to follow a pattern of strong ethnic identification and desire for continuity combined with Americanization and integration, with greater or lesser degrees of assimilation. Some groups, such as the Amish, are famous for sustaining their enclosed communities, with various special rules applying to them to allow them to educate their children in their unique way of life. But most ethnic groups usually engage in American life through newspapers, clubs, and societies, educational initiatives, and active political campaigns. Many Irish-Americans supported Irish independence in the 1920s. Roosevelt complained to Stalin about the influence of the Polish-American lobby. Cuban-Americans have consistently organized and contributed to sustaining the embargo against Castro and the policies around it.

Yet Americans have also shown that where democratic norms and identity have clashed, identity must give way. The territory of Utah was not made a state despite repeated attempts over half a century until the practice of polygamy among its majority Mormons was at least officially renounced by the church. Laws against underage marriage are strictly enforced. Similarly, tough demands are made on those who wish to become citizens of the United States, not only in terms of language skills and civic knowledge but in attesting to loyalty to American principles of democracy.

Native Americans and African-Americans remain emblems of America's failure to integrate distinct groups in its midst. These two groups, it should be noted, did not choose to immigrate to America: the former were already there; most of the latter were forced to come. But these remain the exceptions to the rule. America's successful record of integration is nothing short of staggering.

Muslims too have been notably better integrated in the United States than in Europe. This has occurred, supporters of the veil ban should take note, even though American laws on freedom of expression and religion are more permissive than those in Europe. A Pew Center survey in May 2007 of more than one thousand U.S. Muslims found that seventy-six percent believed their communities were excellent places to live and work, and a higher percentage of Muslims versus non-Muslims were satisfied with the state of the United States. Most striking, forty-seven percent of U.S. Muslims thought of themselves as Muslims first, rather than Americans. This is close to the percentage of U.S. Christians—forty-two percent—and in sharp contrast to British or German Muslims, of whom eighty-one percent and sixty-six percent, respectively, think of themselves as Muslim first.

Testament to the resonance in America of the country's enduring values is that a continuing norm of American political culture, the Revolution included, is to protest not against American ideals but against the failure to live up to them. From Lincoln's fight against slavery to Martin Luther King's struggle against discrimination to the repeated attempts by all parties to refer current public policy issues to the principles of the Constitution, appeals are made to conform to the sacred and enduring values that underpin American life and have shaped American identity for more than two centuries.

IDENTITY STRENGTHENS DEMOCRACY

In the free world, different attitudes toward identity and democracy are reflected in different attitudes toward the crucial questions facing us today. The American model suggests how identity and democracy can be closely allied, in a structure of overlapping identities in which a deep shared commitment to individual rights creates mutual respect. It is different in Europe. Whether the approach has been multicultural, as in Britain and the Netherlands, or assimilationist, as in France, or largely exclusionary, as in Germany, the attitude remains one in which democracy and identity, far from confirming one another, are seen as contradictory impulses. The zero-sum European model, where identity's gain is democracy's loss, remains true today. Unfortunately, European ideas of democracy have left no room for strong identities, and certainly not for different identities each expressing and affirming their own ways of life.

Like a rich mosaic of bright hues that slowly fades into one drab color, European countries, which have done so much to enrich the world with their unique cultures and traditions, are becoming a shell of their former selves in the name of abstract democracy. Europe's loss is no one's gain. In abandoning their traditions and past, the people of Europe will be cut off from the very things that imbue life with purpose and meaning.

But even if Europeans do not place great value in maintaining the particular, Europe's zero-sum view of identity and democracy poses an even more basic question. Can a democratic society that does not make room for identity, let alone nurture strong identities among its citizens, long survive?

Nationalism—the diabolic impulse according to post-identity theories—has been a powerful weapon in defending the free world *against* aggression. Roosevelt, Churchill, and De Gaulle in extremis gave their peoples hope and strength by appealing to history, tradition, and national values. They each drew on their nations' unique past to help secure its future. De Gaulle, as the voice of a free France, declared: "Our only aim, our only interest, is to remain to the end Frenchmen, worthy of France." Churchill reminded his countrymen that beyond "all parties, all creeds, all classes . . . there is one bond which unites us all and sustains us in the public regard, namely that we are prepared to proceed to all extremities, to endure them and to enforce them; that is our bond of union in His Majesty's Government." And in his third inaugural address, nearly a year before Pearl Harbor, FDR, citing George Washington's First Inaugural address, was already appealing to America's past to mobilize the national will for the battle that he knew lay ahead:

> The destiny of America was proclaimed in the world of prophecy spoken by our first president in his First Inaugural of 1789: "the preservation of the sacred fire of liberty and the destiny of the republican model of government are justly considered." If you and I in this later day lose that sacred fire—if we let it be smothered with doubt and fear—then we shall reject the destiny which Washington strove so valiantly and so triumphantly to establish. The preservation of the spirit and faith of the Nation does, and will, furnish the highest justification for every sacrifice that we may make in the cause of national defense.

Each of these leaders in the face of crisis appealed to tradition, to roots, to history, to mutual responsibility in order to protect their community and its values for their children. Time and again throughout history, societies with a strong sense of identity, with groups committed to the preservation of those identities, have been best prepared to unite in efforts to protect and resist threats against them.

Bob Brawer, well-known as a spokesman for homosexual rights and a critic of American Evangelicals for their hostility towards them, recently wrote a book describing how he decided to leave America because of his sense of alienation and his anger at Christian fundamentalists, especially their attitudes towards homosexuals. He felt that he did not want to live among those who rejected him. But what he found was that in Europe, for all its tolerant principles, he was less secure than he was in America. Unwilling to enforce its own values and norms against those Muslim groups who lack democratic traditions, liberal Europe was not able to protect him or guarantee his personal safety. In Brawer's account, *While Europe Slept*, European democrats, instead of clearly rallying around their democratic norms, either ignore the problem, appease those who challenge them, or flee. He writes:

> Given what I had seen of Evangelical Christianity I was
> not upset that Christian belief in Western Europe had
> declined precipitously. But then I saw that when Christian
> faith had departed it had taken with it a sense of
> ultimate meaning and purpose and left the Continent

vulnerable to conquest by people with deeper faith and stronger convictions. And no longer able to take religion seriously themselves they were unable to believe that other people might take religion seriously indeed.

Democracy requires passion: passion to organize, to mobilize, to participate, to persuade, to get people involved and energized to fight for what they believe in. This passion comes from deep attachments. Identity provides those attachments.

Individual rights are fundamental to a democratic society, but community life is fundamental to individuals. The self is deeply dependent on the worlds out of which it has emerged. Each person is born into a family, into a community, into a history that binds them with ties and gives them a sense of who they are beyond the mere self. This kind of belonging creates the cohesion and obligation that all societies depend on, for care as well as for defense.

Identity strengthens that sense of self that serves as the building block for self-government. The way to strengthen society is not to weaken an individual's sense of self. It was precisely on this point that Aristotle criticized his revered teacher Plato. The latter dreamed of a utopian Republic where particular attachments, most prominently the family, were wiped away in the name of strengthening attachments to the state. To Plato, attachments were a zero-sum game. Aristotle disagreed. To him, a man could be a good father and a good patriot. In fact, the former was critical to the latter. Strong families build stronger communities, which build stronger nations.

EVANGELICAL CHRISTIANS

The fear of identity is not confined to Europe. In America, many liberals fear and distrust Evangelical Christians, seeing them as a threat to democracy. They believe that the Evangelicals are challenging long-standing arrangements in the separation between church and state and the safeguards that have been developed to prevent a particular identity from imposing itself on others.

I have met many American Evangelicals. Their relationship to Jews and to Israel is to some surprising, but it has a long history. The Puritans strongly identified with the Hebrew Scripture of the Old Testament. They saw their journey to the New World as going to a new promised land. Moreover, America lacks a history of persecution of Jews. Nevertheless, much distrust and fear is felt by Jews toward Evangelicals. The history of suspicion and indeed hostility of the Christian church against Jews, missionary activity, and a traditional denial of the legitimacy of Jewish religious life provide the Jews with well-founded reasons to distrust activist Christians, whose support today still often includes a vision of the final conversion of the Jews in preparation for the Second Coming of the Messiah.

However, in attending many rallies of Evangelicals in support of Israel, I could not but be impressed by their level of devotion, by the number of Israeli flags in evidence, something that is unimaginable anywhere else in the world. When Evangelicals speak about common roots and shared passion about God, I see many of my American-Jewish friends grow uncomfortable and suspicious. Don't you understand, they tell me: Even if they don't want to turn us into Christians here and now, they support Israel only as the way to bring the Second Coming and the final redemption. But I argue in return: Why does that matter? At least until the Messiah comes, we and the Evangelicals share common ground. When that fateful day arrives, we can resolve our dispute by simply asking the Messiah whether he has been here before. But until then, when we have mutual enemies, when antidemocratic fundamentalist Islam is threatening not only Israel but all free societies, let us work together for the benefit of all.

The sense of mutual cooperation I share with Evangelicals is a by-product of my own past. The Pentecostals in the Soviet Union were prohibited from teaching their religion, persecuted remorselessly, exiled, and moved deeper and deeper into Siberia, all the way to the border of China and Japan, and even there were not left alone. As unofficial spokesman for the dissident movement, I helped their leaders make their first contact with foreign journalists in Moscow in the mid-1970s. When I was arrested, thousands fasted and prayed for my release and my freedom. In prison I came to the conclusion that people with strong identities are the best potential allies. The same is true in free societies. Obviously, such an alliance will demand a commitment to the core principles of democratic life. But those who champion those democratic principles but have weak identities will, as was true in prison, ultimately prove unreliable. After all, who is better prepared to confront challenges? Those with strong identities who accept democracy or staunch democrats who reject identity as a kind of prejudice? Which society is stronger? A society of people devoted to their own identities and respectful of the rights of others to express their identities or a society of cosmopolitans whose utopian vision is a world without barriers but also without deep connections or particular commitments that might be a source of strife? It is surely better to have a society armed with strong identities framed by democracy than a society of strong democrats indifferent to identity. Indeed, the best defense of the free world will come from those who cherish a unique way of life, for they will always have a life truly worth defending.

CHAPTER 6

Altneuland: *At the Crossroads of Identity and Democracy*

CONTEMPORARY DEBATES over the origins of nationalism claim that nations are an invention of the last few hundred years. But the Jews have been a nation for three thousand years, defying simple definitions, sustaining themselves throughout the centuries only by maintaining a strong identity. Although their history stretches from ancient to modern times, Jews were scattered all over the world for two thousand years. Stalin was correct when he said that Jews, lacking a political state, a mutual economic life, or even a shared geographic location, were not appropriate or suitable to ordinary national definitions. Arnold Toynbee, unable to make sense of the permanence of this stateless people, infamously referred to the Jews as a "fossil" of history.

But at the same time, the Jews' connection as a people has been as real as that of any other people. They experienced their history practically every day, united by reading the books of the Bible and its commentaries, which became the source of their ethics, their laws, their prayers and dreams. Dispersed all over the world, they spoke different languages, followed different traditions, becoming an integral part of different countries and states. But they continued to consider themselves one people. Along the way, many Jews were lost through persecution and through destruction and later, when the gates of the outside world were opened to them, through assimilation. But whatever trials they faced, the march of the Jews through the centuries as one people continued, with a deep and abiding sense of purpose. As Paul Johnson, the British historian and commentator, has said, "No people have insisted more firmly than the Jews that history has a purpose and humanity a destiny." For the Jews, this joint life as a nation has undergone a profound and dramatic transformation as they emerged from two thousand years of wandering to build a homeland in which they can find political as well as cultural expression as a nation.

If you glance at almost any Western newspaper, you would think from the sheer volume of headlines and front page coverage that Israel was a country of vast territory inhabited by tens of millions, if not hundreds of millions, of people. A Chinese person once asked, "Why does the world hear so much about Israel when there are only fifty million of you?" Well, his question is even more apt than he thought because

Israel is smaller than New Jersey and has a population of little more than seven million people. So why then is there so much focus on Israel?

Israel is a country founded on identity. It is also a country whose birth and survival were made possible only through democracy. To gather together a people scattered across the world for two millennia to renew their sovereign national existence could happen only with voluntary commitment, with the passion and energy that comes from free men and women devoted to living together, working together, and defending their new nation together.

This coming together of democracy and identity—with the many challenges and strains it involves—puts Israel in the center of the confrontation between these two forces in the wider world. Geographically, Israel is a democratic country situated in the middle of totalitarian, dictatorial, and authoritarian regimes. Culturally, it is a Jewish country in the middle of the Arab and Islamic world. Politically, it is a nation-state committed to preserving a national and ethnic identity in a world where post-identity ideologies are on the ascendant. In a time of post-modernity, most of its people share an ancient identity reconstituted in a modern state. Moreover, Israel is deeply tied to European history and Europe's attempts to come to terms with that history. It is part of the West and therefore subject to the same forces that are creating a crisis of identity throughout the West. At the same time, it is part of the Middle East. It straddles the seam that pits radical Islam against modernity and the West. As the center of the Jewish nation, Israel is of fundamental importance not only to Jewish history but to Western culture as well. It has been, and remains, like the proverbial canary in the coal mine, a leading indicator of the dangers, issues, crises, and concerns that threaten the West as a whole.

Questions of democracy and identity were foremost in the minds of those who established the state. Many people assume Israel has an exclusive, monolithic identity. But Israel is in fact composed of many ethnic groups, including not only many types of Christians and Muslims, Druze and Bahai, but also many kinds of Jews from many parts of the world, each with their own customs, histories, traditions, and practices.

For a host of reasons, Israel is a fascinating laboratory to test the tension between democracy and identity. It is both the only democracy in the Middle East as well as a Jewish nation-state. How these two notions are to work together is a daily test of Israel's integrity and indeed its survival. Israel faces a number of immense challenges, each one of which requires a monumental effort to address: It was born out of traumatized European Jewry and also had to absorb quickly the hundreds of thousands of Jews who were driven out of Arab countries in the aftermath of Israel's independence. It needed to attract and absorb huge numbers of Jews from many diverse places and countries. It needed to create (and still does create) out of this diversity a living, breathing Jewish culture that is also modern, tolerant, and democratic. It defines itself as a Jewish state that is dedicated to guaranteeing equal rights to all its citizens. It is surrounded by non-democratic countries that reject its right to existence and specifically its Jewish identity. Each of these challenges is daunting in itself and places enormous strain on Israel. Yet without a commitment to both democracy and identity, the State of Israel cannot long survive.

In the great effort to build the State of Israel, the issue of identity looms large. First and foremost, the question of the proper place for identity in Israeli society has played a critical role in determining the character of the Jewish state, as well as its relations with Jews around the world. Second, identity has been central to the shifting attitudes toward the idea of a Jewish state in the international community and even to Israeli attitudes toward their own country. Third, different views about the importance of identity have had a profound effect on Israel's still elusive quest for peace with its neighbors. Put simply, Israel is a stage on which the drama of identity in the modern world is played out each and every day.

JEWISH-ISRAELI IDENTITIES: BUILDING THE STATE

The global debate about the role of identity discussed in previous chapters in many ways comes down to the question of whether identities that create meaningful differences in society are primarily a source of strength or a source of conflict and war. To strengthen society, is it necessary to erase identities, to reduce them in a "melting pot" that turns all identities into one? Or can different identities be framed by democracy to become linked identities in which there is room for their full expression not only in private but also in a shared public space? The answer to this question became crucial in the process of building the State of Israel.

Groups of religious Jews have always lived in what is now Israel and many more have always dreamt of living there, facing and blessing Jerusalem in their thrice-daily prayers, mourning the destruction of the *Beit Hamikdash* (Solomon's ancient temple) that once stood there, remembering Jerusalem when they marry off their children, and pledging every Passover, "Next year in Jerusalem." But the idea of creating a Jewish state as the only political solution that could save the Jews from catastrophe was advanced in modern times by a secular, assimilated Austrian Jew, Theodore Herzl. Herzl's idea of the Jewish state was born out of a sense of impending doom, and its central purpose was to provide a safe haven. Herzl was truly prophetic. Witnessing the spontaneous outburst of anti-Semitism at the Dreyfus trial in Paris, he foresaw a future Holocaust. He wrote of the coming calamity in his diary:

> I cannot imagine what appearance and form this will take. Will it be expropriation by some revolutionary force from below? Will it be proscription by some reactionary force from above? Will they banish us? Will they kill us? I expect all these forms and others.

Herzl anticipated both the revolutionary forces of Marxism and the fascistic forces of Hitler. He wrote elsewhere: "The longer it takes to come, the worse it will be . . . there is no escaping it." His feeling of an imminent disaster drove him on.

Herzl believed that hatred toward Jews was due to Jews being seen as a separate people. Exactly because of their commitment to their own collective history, Jews were resented and rejected by others in a way that, as the Dreyfus case showed, could surface at any moment. Herzl also saw in this national, collective identity the power that drove the Jewish people to survive and that would impel them towards their own political independence. He wrote in *The Jewish State*:

> The distinctive nationality of Jews neither can, will, nor must be destroyed. It cannot be destroyed, because external enemies consolidate it. It will not be destroyed: this is shown during two thousand years of appalling suffering. It must not be destroyed, and that, as a descendent of numberless Jews who refused to despair, I am trying once more to prove in this pamphlet.

In one day, he changed his life: from professional journalist to messiah of the Jewish state. He traveled around the globe, met with world leaders, visited far-flung Jewish communities, and most importantly, created the political movement of Zionism. Yet tragically, others did not heed his warnings in time and his rescue mission failed. Disaster soon overtook European Jewry.

Herzl passed away in 1904, eight years after he began his quest. But the movement he began would establish a

Jewish state less than fifty years after his death (this too, he predicted). It was left to David Ben-Gurion and his Zionist Socialist comrades to build the state Herzl envisioned.

But Herzl's vision of Jewish identity was different from Ben-Gurion's. Herzl believed that the future had to be rooted in the past. He repeatedly emphasized the central role that classical Jewish identity would play in the reconstituted national identity of the Jewish people. "Zionism," he declared at the First Zionist Congress in 1897, "is a return to the Jewish fold, even before it becomes a return to the Jewish land." Although he himself grew up with almost no connection to religion, Herzl recognized the importance of religion as part of Jewish culture and history, and thereby an important link between all Jews: "We identify ourselves as a people on account of our religion," he wrote in his journal. Elsewhere he wrote: "Our community of race is peculiar and unique, for we are bound together only by the faith of our fathers." In his imagined state, the Altneuland, or new-old land, he envisions rabbis as "supporting pillars" and synagogues "in every neighborhood, visible from long distances, for it is only our ancient faith that has kept us together."

Therefore, far from being indifferent to Jewish cultural roots, he knew that the revival of Jewish national life had to be connected to the Jews' own sense of history, of culture, of who they were and are and hoped to be. In Herzl's vision, the restored Jewish homeland would also be inclusive and pluralistic. All the diverse Diaspora experiences, all the different cultural forms that Jews had encountered and adopted during their two-thousand-year exile, would be brought with them to Israel and become part of the new state. "We will give a home to our people," he wrote,

> not by dragging them ruthlessly out of their sustaining soil, but rather by transplanting them carefully to better ground. Just as we wish to create new political and economic relations, so we shall preserve as sacred all of the past that is dear to our people's hearts.

Each would bring to the new-old land their own histories and knowledge, would continue to be "in the new country what we are [in our native countries], and we shall never cease to cherish with sadness the memory of the native land out of which we have been driven." The resulting image is one that emphasizes a core, common, and shared Jewishness as the center of identity, but which also has many spokes that lead to—and also away from—the diversity of cultures the Jews had experienced. To use Herzl's own metaphor, the Altneuland would be a garden of many different plants, carefully replanted in this new and better soil. All would be transplanted to the new country to create what he called a "Mosaic mosaic," a rich mix of already existing Jewish cultures, ancient and modern, diverse yet joined in the enterprising spirit of nation building.

The Israel that Ben-Gurion and his comrades envisioned had different origins and different principles. His generation had missed the awful pogroms during the first (1905) and second (1917) revolutions in Russia. A number of different

parties and movements in one way or another connected to
Marxism were fighting at the time against the Tsarist
regime: Communists, Socialists, social revolutionaries, and
so on. Jews, whose lives under the Tsars were at best uncertain and at worst in constant peril, were active in each of
these movements. On the other hand, the World Zionist
movement created by Herzl in 1897 enjoyed broad support
from the Jewish community living under Tsarist rule, which
was by far the biggest Jewish community and probably the
most oppressed in the world at that time.

At first glance, it would seem that Zionism and socialism are inherently incompatible. After all, didn't Marx and
Engels proclaim that the proletariat has no motherland and
that only the international class struggle of the proletariat
could pave the way to communism? For many Jews, however, the building of a classless society was an aim for the
distant future while the present reality was one of horrifying pogroms. As one of the major theoreticians of socialist
Zionism, Nahman Sirkin, wrote: "Socialism with its basic
principles of peace, cooperation and cultural progress
bears the seed out of which pure internationalism, that is,
cosmopolitanism will develop. . . . But socialism will solve
the Jewish problem only in the remote future." The violence of the pogroms impressed Ben-Gurion's generation of
Socialist Jews no less then the Dreyfus trial had impressed
Herzl. An immediate solution was needed and Zionism
offered it. The interests of Jews as the most oppressed
nationality and the proletariat as the most oppressed and
revolutionary class were united in the dream of building

socialism in what was then called Palestine. For the Zionist Socialist pioneers, establishing a Jewish state would be an important step on the way to the victory of the world socialist international.

But the socialist vision, especially Russian socialism in the second half of the nineteenth century, demanded more than a new society based on social justice. It demanded a "new man" who would transform humanity and create a just society abiding by new moral principles. The idea of a new man who would reject the norms and morals of the old world and build a new life in a new world was a central idea in *What to Do*, a book by the early Russian Socialist Nikolay Chernyshevsky. In Lenin's famous expression, this book "turned over the soil" in the souls of a generation of socialist revolutionaries. Among Zionist Socialists this idea manifested itself in the image of the "New Jew."

Herzl's vision was built on and out of thousands of years that had sustained the Jews in exile. No new identity would displace the old or be imposed upon it. Any changes would come through democratic processes and voluntary effort. But the idea of the new Jew that Ben-Gurion and his colleagues brought with them from Russia was revolutionary. Ben-Gurion's socialist ideal was of a person who disconnects himself from the past—a past that is seen as two thousand years of humiliation and slavery—and takes fate into his own hands. In this way, the Jewish *Yishuv* (settlement in Israel) became popular both to those who believed in a national Jewish state and to those who in the name of the new socialist utopia wanted to break from past Jewish identities. Many in this group saw the Jewish state as their path to the utopian world of communism.

Herzl's vision of a "Mosaic mosaic" was one where each individual would bring his own cultural experience, even his own language, to contribute to the making of a society at once rooted and modern. Ben-Gurion, in contrast, spoke of "the integration of Diaspora Jewry into one homogeneous Hebrew brigade." To him, Israeli identity would come out of the crucible of the melting pot. Ben-Gurion spoke of the "Jewish dust" out of which the *Sabra*—the new Jew—would be molded. He called for new Hebrew forms of culture and festivals, for the abandonment of European-sounding names for Hebrew ones. For two thousand years, the Jews had no state, no army, no economy, no responsibility for the collective safety of their people. Its history was instead one of pogroms and of attempts by prominent Jews to curry favor with one ruler after another, who were often capricious dictators whose attitudes toward the Jews could change at any moment. To Ben-Gurion, therefore, meaningful Jewish history skipped from the Bible's account of Jewish independence and heroism (exemplified by Kind David and the Macabees) straight to Zionism:

> There has been a profound and fundamental change in the lives of hundreds and thousands of Jews here . . . a wholesale revolution in a Jew's image and his way of life . . . on the trunk of ancient Hebrew culture the prospect of a new Hebrew culture is sprouting . . . a transformation of man [that] happens to all who return to Zion.

Masada, the mountaintop where Jews in the first century made their famous final stand against the Romans and decided to commit suicide rather than surrender, became the sacred space to which pilgrimages would be made and where inspiring ceremonies of initiation into the newly founded Israeli army took place (and still do).

Ben-Gurion faced formidable challenges, and his centralized approach no doubt played an important role in founding and preserving the new nation. The young Jewish communities of Palestine were under constant attack. Forces of self-defense had to be organized by people who for centuries had never had political or military experience. The British, who had been given by the League of Nations after World War I a mandate over Palestine that called for "establishing a Jewish national home" there, broke the terms of that mandate by preventing Jews from escaping a Europe turning fascist and violent against them. Bringing these Jews to Palestine became the most pressing issue for the Jewish community in Palestine, and all resources of the community were mobilized and devoted to the vast underground operation of smuggling Jews into Israel. This effort, which no doubt required centralized decision making, became an important part of the new identity: To bring Jews to Israel meant fulfilling your mission. Every Jew who arrived was considered a success for Zionism. But Ben-Gurion's efforts at building a new people extended well beyond the exigencies of that perilous time. The ideology of the new Jew became a founding aspect of the fledgling state; it was taught in schools, promoted in government institutions, and became a central value of public culture.

Ben-Gurion's notion of the new Jew, for all its Zionist commitment, was problematic. It was deeply paternalistic. It implied that he would define who that Jew should be. He knew what was needed, what had to be changed. Embracing Jewish immigrants who survived the destruction of European Jewry and the hundreds and thousands of Jews who were forced to flee Arab countries was one of the most pioneering, romantic, and formative moments of the state. In two or three years, the Jewish population in Israel doubled. Yet the largely Russian-born Ashkenazi Jews—the secular and Socialist Jews then ruling the state—felt that they knew best where these newcomers should live and work, what kind of education their children should get, and what way of life they should follow. For the Sephardic Jews, this meant abandoning traditional customs they had observed for centuries, if not millennia, and fraying some of their ties to religion. For some, it meant nothing less than abandoning their unique identity.

In this way the Zionist project, while welcoming and absorbing immigrants and doing everything to bring them to Israel and integrate them into society, also adopted socialist models, which meant deciding what kind of identity the newcomers would have and who they would be.

During that same time, official ideology in the Soviet Union was trying to turn citizens into "Homo Sovieticus," seeing them as a "cog" in the communist machine. It is not a coincidence that, albeit to very different ends, two states were trying to redefine the identity of their citizens from above. A critical difference separated the project to build a new Soviet man by *enforced* communism from the project to build a new Jew by *voluntary* Zionism. Soviet socialism involved the confiscation of property and exiling, enslaving, and killing tens of millions. Collective farms were a horrific failure that caused millions of people to starve to death. In contrast, Zionist socialism established voluntary democratic communities (*kibbutzim*) that survived through the twentieth century and were the longest lasting—if ultimately failed—communist experiments in history. The same can be said about any other institution in democratic Israel compared to totalitarian Soviet Union. For all their paternalism, Israeli leaders, unlike Soviet leaders, could be voted out.

And that is exactly what happened. The Soviet Union disintegrated because of the inner weakness of the regime and its attempts to keep under control the lives and brains of two hundred million people. In Israel, the attempts to impose a new identity were undermined by the democratic process itself. In the end it was the union of the traditional ideological opposition to the dominant Labor Party and the movement of Sephardic Jews, angry at what they perceived as decades of paternalism from that same Labor Party toward them, that came together in the elections of 1977 and ended the thirty-year socialist monopoly on political power in Israel.

Despite this political setback for Ben-Gurion's ideological heirs, the paternalistic approach towards the new immigrants persisted in Israel's absorption policies. One strong blow against that melting pot model came with a new wave of Russian *aliyah* (immigration) in the 1990s.

LINKED JEWISH IDENTITIES: THE RUSSIAN ALIYAH

The democratic process had been undermining the ideology of the melting pot as time went on, but the arrival of a massive wave of immigrants from the former Soviet Union dealt it a final blow. When the iron curtain was brought down, over one million Soviet Jews arrived in Israel in less than a decade—the equivalent of sixty million new immigrants arriving in the United States in a similar time frame. The members of this *aliyah* were highly educated and highly ambitious. Soviet Jews, experiencing state discrimination, saw higher education as the best means of survival and were therefore driven to excel in science, mathematics, technology, and the arts. When they arrived in Israel, the number of doctors, engineers, and mathematicians in the country doubled in only a few years, while the number of musicians and chess players increased exponentially.

Soviet Jews knew from their own deep experience how bad it was to be deprived of one's identity. Having been forced to live for three generations without identity, many came to Israel hoping to find one. The model of the new Jew, a creation that lacked history or cultural ties to the past, was therefore one they could not accept. One immigrant expressed to me what many others were thinking: "I thought in coming to Israel I would add three thousand years of history. Instead, I lost thirty. The Soviets began history in 1917. In Israel, it begins in 1948."

These immigrants wanted to embrace their new life in Israel but also wanted to remain Jews infused with a rich, Russian culture. They kept their language, insisted on highly competitive education, organized many self-support groups, and took an active role in political life, eventually forming their own party (of which I was elected chairman). Through determination and energy they opened the doors of an Israeli society that had once been closed to newcomers. The ethos espoused by Israel's Socialist founders was that the first generation of newcomers would be like the "generation of the desert." Invoking the image of the Jews who left Egypt and wandered for forty years in the Sinai before coming to the promised land, only the immigrants' children, who had grown up in Israel, could become full members of the society.

But the Russian immigrants wanted to enter the promised land directly. Second-class citizens their entire life, they wanted to be equal citizens right away. The slogan for the first and very successful elections of the Russian party, which I led in 1996, was "there is no integration without representation." At the national level, the new immigrant party won 7 seats (out of 120) in the Israeli Knesset, enabling it to play a pivotal role in Israel's fractured political system, where government coalitions rule by small majorities. At the municipal level, hundreds of new immigrants took seats on city councils and in city government, where the real integration was taking place—in schools, in the workplace, and in communities.

At issue were not only different attitudes toward *aliyah* and integration but different conceptions of Israeli society itself. It was about the possibility of a society comprised, as Herzl had imagined, of a diversity of cultural attachments and interests, with each group bringing their own experience into a "Mosaic mosaic" of Israel, while still committed to a Jewish identity that would connect everyone.

The Gesher Theater is a small but characteristic example of how this pluralistic vision changed the pattern of building identities in Israel. At the beginning of the large wave of immigration in 1990, I received a call from some famous Moscow theater producers and actors who were Jewish. At the time, I was the head of the Soviet Jewry Zionist Forum, a new organization created by new immigrants, of new immigrants, and for new immigrants, which initiated and supported projects of integration. The Russian theater people told me they were interested in immigration, but they wanted to know whether there would be any possibility of their working and performing in Israel. That is, would there be any opportunity or support for some type of Russian-language theater?

I thought this was a terrific idea. It would be good for theatergoers but more importantly good for *aliyah* itself. Here was a way to attract to Israel part of the Jewish Russian intelligentsia, cultural leaders whose arrival would encourage and send a message to many others that they would be coming to a place where they could feel at home.

I was sure that this enthusiasm would be shared by the Israeli authorities. But I was shocked by the reaction the idea received. I went to the leaders of the theater community and to the Ministry of Education and Culture in Israel with the idea of opening an Israeli-Russian theater. They were adamantly opposed. They told me that they had never agreed to theaters in other languages, not Romanian, not Bulgarian, not even in Yiddish. Hebrew was needed to promote unity in the country. The miracle of Hebrew's rebirth from its long centuries as an effectively dead language could not be challenged or put at risk. "Don't you as a Zionist," they asked me, "recognize the miracle of bringing a dead language back to life? We need to strengthen the connection between Hebrew and the Jewish people. Everyone who comes here has to learn the language. What you are asking for will prevent newcomers from becoming part of Israel."

The rebirth of Hebrew is indeed a miracle and essential to creating a common culture. It is in all senses a unique revolution in history. But I thought Zionism strong enough not only to preserve and recreate the past but also to include new forms. And I felt that what was important was to give Russian immigrants a platform for self-expression and for contributing to Israel's cultural richness according to Herzl's image of transplanting rather than uprooting immigrants. It was a concrete way to convince other Russian Jews that they would have a place here. So I set out to raise money elsewhere from people who would be more sympathetic. The Jewish Federation of New York contributed money to fund a few concerts, and the Zionist Forum raised enough to cover the theater's first-year budget.

What has emerged is a fantastic success story. At first, only Russian immigrants came to the performances. But eventually actors began performing in Hebrew as well. The Gesher Theater—which means "bridge"—now features Russian speakers acting in Hebrew and Hebrew speakers acting in Russian. Children are brought from Israeli schools to see theater of the highest quality. This is a cultural, an economic, and also a Zionist contribution to Israeli life. The Gesher Theater has received more international awards than any other Israeli theater.

What the Russian *aliyah* shows is that there is an alternate way to build identity, not as a melting pot but rather, as Herzl envisioned, as a mosaic, where a public space is created for different groups to express fully their unique identities. Although there are Russian-language newspapers, television, and radio, the effect is not separation. Instead, it has helped connect new arrivals to their new culture and has made them less likely to suffer traumatic periods of frustration and isolation in a new country. When these Jews first arrived, many feared that this very assimilated *aliyah*, disconnected from its Jewish roots by years of Soviet denial of them, would bring assimilation to Israel. But in fact, it has brought Israeli society closer to Diaspora Jewry, through a large number of people who, like me, feel themselves at the same time to be part of both Israel and the Diaspora. A sweet irony to this story is that the Israeli melting pot approach created on the eve of the Russian revolution by Russian Jews was transformed dramatically four generations later by Russian immigrants who arrived after the collapse of the USSR.

Russian *aliyah* and its integration, despite all criticisms and difficulties, has been a huge success. Israeli society has surmounted this enormous challenge, but it has done so by strengthening hyphenation, not erasing it; by inviting linkages among identities, not eliminating them. Israeli culture is nothing more than an abstraction without the concrete and particular cultures and histories that make it up, be they Moroccan, Russian, Yemeni, French, or American. Culture cannot function without history. To erase these particulars is to erase culture itself.

To be Russian-Jewish is then to be one sort of Israeli, alongside many others: American-Jewish-Israeli; Moroccan-Jewish-Israeli; Yemenite-Jewish-Israeli; French-Jewish-, British-Jewish-, German-Jewish-Israeli. An astonishing feature of Israeli life is the enormous variety of kinds of Jews who have come to Israel. In the area where I live in Jerusalem, in the two or three streets surrounding me, there are many different synagogues: Moroccan, Turkish, English, French, and many others. In the café near my house, one can meet American high-tech specialists, French pharmacists, and Russian doctors who all seem to emerge straight out of Herzl's dreams. The different backgrounds create diversity. What joins them—linking them to each other while they maintain their own different pasts and traditions—is Jewish culture.

Ultra-Orthodox disciples of the *Gaon* (genius) from Vilna who immigrated to the Land of Israel in the eighteenth century, Zionist Socialists at the end of the nineteenth century, and assimilated Jews from Soviet Russia who fought for their right to immigrate at the end of the twentieth century had nothing in common with regard to their perception of the Jewish tradition. However, all of them saw themselves as partners in the realization of the same ancient dream to return to the Land of Israel and to fulfill their people's timeworn prayer "to renew our days as of old."

WORLDS OF JEWISH IDENTITY

The paternalistic socialist approach of the founding fathers in creating a new Israeli identity caused two types of problems: one in relations between Israelis and new immigrants and the other in relations between Israel and Diaspora Jews. The first was eventually checked by the democratic character of Israeli society.

The division between Israeli and traditional Diaspora forms of Jewish identity is much more complex. Here, democracy does not provide a mechanism of change. Instead, deep opposing views of identity clash head on. The extent to which the powerful internal forces that have preserved Jewish identity throughout history will retain their potency when that identity is transformed into an Israeli identity depends on how much the new Israeli identity is rooted in Jewish history. It is precisely this rootedness that those who espoused the ideology of the new Jew tried to eliminate.

The tension over this issue was brought to the surface on the occasion of A. B. Yehoshua's address to the American Jewish Committee's annual meeting (May 1–2, 2006) at the celebration of their one hundredth anniversary. Invited as an expression of the American Jewish community's pride in Israeli intellectuals and in Israel as a nation, Yehoshua, a world-renowned Israeli writer, told his audience in Washington, D.C., something deeply disturbing:

My identity is Israeli, which is the true Jewish identity. It is based in geography, language, and Israeli institutions—the territory, the smell of the territory, the smell of the language—all this is my identity. . . . To speak Hebrew defines my cultural identity; to live in Israel, my national one. Outside of these it is impossible to have a Jewish identity of any significance.

Yehoshua's American hosts were shocked. They saw Israelis as an important expression of their own Jewishness, even their own avant-garde; as pioneers who were realizing a vision that was part of their own life. Yet here Yehoshua was divorcing Israel from the Diaspora Jews, from a common Jewish heritage, from three thousand years of culture, creativity, prayer, rituals, tradition, and everything that is subsumed in the term Judaism.

But Yehoshua's words should not come as a surprise. They are in fact the logical culmination of Ben-Gurion's vision of the new Jew that would found a new nation. He painted an image of an Israeli nation as if it arose magically from the sea one hundred years ago. For Yehoshua—and many others in Israel—the only thing that is important, existential, and relevant from the Jewish perspective is what happens in Israel. The centuries before the modern return to Zion and life outside Zion are irrelevant. And the Israeli self-definition as the new Jew leaves little room for ties to communities of Diaspora Jews who remain Jewish culturally and religiously but who do not live in Israel.

In the many responses to Yehoshua's speech, the authors were concerned with its meaning for and effect on the Jews of the Diaspora. But in my response I emphasized my concern for what this position means for Israeli identity itself:

> The discussion of our right to the land and the war between our narrative and theirs is not a purely philosophical discussion. At least not in the eyes of the Palestinian leaders. When the leaders of Hamas, like Yasser Arafat in his day, were or are prepared to consider recognition of the fact of Israel's existence, but not its right to existence, they are not playing word games. That is why Arafat reiterated over and over again his supposedly historical claims with regard to the absence of the connection between the Temple Mount and the Jewish people. It was clear to him that the historical connection that is anchored and based in Jewish tradition is the basis for the existence of the State of Israel, and without it, the state will disappear, just as it "appeared from the sea."
>
> The difference between Israeli identity according to Yehoshua and Jewish identity is exactly the difference between the fact of existence and the right to exist. The difference is between a group of people that lives on a piece of land and speaks the Hebrew language, and the descendants of a people that is scattered throughout the world, who have returned to their historic homeland.
>
> If, heaven forbid, we cut ourselves off from the chain that links us to the Jewish people, if we cut ourselves off from three thousand years of Judaism, if we cut ourselves off from being the realization of two thousand years of Jewish hope—for next year in Jerusalem—then

we will lose the right to our existence. And in losing that right, we will be lost.

Perhaps the Jews of the Diaspora were insulted by Yehoshua's blunt remarks, but we, the Jews of the Land of Israel, we must rise up against them, for this is a matter of the very fact of our existence.

As soon as we separate ourselves from world Jewry and turn ourselves into new Jews, whose history begins only from the moment the modern State of Israel was created, the theory of Israel as a colonial power gains currency, not only for others but for Israelis themselves.

Many years ago in Moscow in some of the most intense moments of my activities as a Jewish dissident, one American tourist told me: You look and act like a real *Sabra*. I took this as a great compliment. Israel was for us a source of strength and the beacon of hope. Our fates were inextricably connected to theirs.

But since I arrived in Israel I feel myself more and more to be a Jew of the Diaspora. I have drawn strength from my connection with Jewish history, from my people's enduring commitment to our unique identity. My statements at government meetings to the effect that Israel belongs to all the Jews of the world and not only to Israelis were often met by my colleagues with amazement and puzzlement. My statements on the Diaspora, that for those who want to influence the future of the Jewish people, the best place is Israel, have not always been welcomed by my audience, and my remarks on university campuses of the continuing importance of

Israel to Jewish identity in America and in the world have often been met with incomprehension. With time, this opposition between old and new, between an ancient Jewish history and a modern Jewish statehood, has come to seem to me more and more invalid. I personally cannot divide myself into an old Jew and a new Jew. It is a false choice. The new Jew created in one phase of Israeli history, regardless of its potential merits, I hope will be consigned, like the Marxist ideology that spawned it, to the dustbin of history.

Shulamit Aloni, a former Israeli minister of education who was the chairman of the dovish political party Meretz, defended Yehoshua this way: "I am an Israeli without hyphens. Here, there is no duality of identity like that among Jews abroad."

But what Mrs. Aloni apparently does not recognize is that these hyphens give meaning and purpose to Israeli life. The line she so casually dismisses is the line that reaches out to our fellow Jews all over the world, reaches back to all the generations of Jews who yearned to return to Zion, and stretches forward to link all Jews together in a common destiny.

CHAPTER 7

Defending the Nation-State

IN OCTOBER 2003 the European Commission conducted a poll to investigate the attitudes of citizens in fifteen European countries to various other countries around the world. The results were so appalling that for some time the poll's sponsors in Brussels were hesitant to publish it. After 9/11, at a time when Al Qaeda was blackmailing the world and threatening more suicide attacks, when Iran was developing a nuclear capability, and when intelligence services in Europe were warning about a broadening network of international terror taking root there, poll respondents ranked America as a greater threat to the world than Iran, North Korea, or Afghanistan. But one country was regarded as even more dangerous than America: Fully fifty-nine percent of those questioned considered Israel the number one threat to world peace and security.

These attitudes, however irrational, are becoming widely accepted. Hatred towards America is often accompanied by hatred towards Israel, whether by the leaders of Iran and Al Qaeda, who speak of the Great and Little Satan, or by the intelligentsia of post-identity Europe, where of all the "bad identities," America and Israel are cited as the worst.

But there is one important difference in the attitudes toward these two supposed rogue nations. America, it is thought, must merely be reined in. Israel must be destroyed. This is declared openly by the leaders of Iran but also, albeit in less strident tones and in more subtle ways, by the ideological proponents of a post-identity world. That Israel is no longer regarded as having a moral right to exist is something you hear more and more often. The United Nations Commission on Human Rights condemned Israel for human rights violations more than it did all the world's dictatorships put together. When criticized for this approach and finally disbanded, it was replaced by a new Council that immediately decided to suspend all discussion of repression in Cuba, Belorussia, and China and to restrict the discussion of Sudan and other countries of Africa where genocide is taking place. The only country that would be placed on the permanent agenda and subjected to constant scrutiny was Israel. The World Conference Against Racism at Durban in 2001 made its central interest not a misogynist Saudi Arabia nor a genocidal Sudan nor a totalitarian North Korea but rather Israel, seeing it as the ultimate racist state, recalling the earlier UN Resolution on "Zionism as Racism" and causing the United States and Israel to walk out.

Why this strange obsession with Israel? Why is it so hated? Why, alone among nations, is even its right to exist brought into question?

Some believe that hostile attitudes toward Israel are merely a function of its misguided policies. Change the policies, the argument goes, and the hatred toward Israel will melt away. According to this view, if the Israeli "occupation" of 1967 ends and the Palestinian refugee issue from 1948 is resolved—two wounds that ostensibly must be healed—an Israel that has become a pariah of the international community will be brought back to its bosom. But it is not true.

The case against Israel is weak. There were wars to destroy Israel before 1967, when Israel received scant support from the international community in defending itself. The PLO was founded in 1964 to liberate a Palestine that at the time included none of what today is commonly called the occupied territories. Exactly what Palestine were the PLO and their Arab supporters trying to liberate when they were calling for the Jews to be thrown into the sea? Similarly, the refugees, who have indeed suffered greatly, have their own Palestinian leadership and Arab brothers to blame for not resettling them as Jews did to the hundreds of thousands of Jewish refugees who were driven out of Arab lands during that same time period.

So something else is going on behind the objection to Israel's continued possession of the territory gained in 1967. The treatment of Israel in the international community, the constant opprobrium it receives, the rage and animosity directed at it do not equate with the depth of the dispute over the 1967 borders, no matter how seriously you take that issue. After all, the Chinese have occupied Tibet for nearly fifty years and no one has suggested that this occupation brings into question China's right to exist. Likewise, tens of millions were displaced in Africa, Asia, and Europe in the last century, but this has never raised questions about the legitimacy of the countries from which they were expelled or were forced to flee.

To make sense of the unique hostility toward Israel in an age when the likes of Kim Il Jung and Mahmood Ahmadinejad roam the earth, one must take a different view. One must see the Jewish state as singularly evil, a near-satanic force that undermines the peace and tranquility of the world and must be eliminated. There is a name for such a view. It is what historian Robert Wistrich has called the longest hatred in the world: anti-Semitism.*

ANTI-JEWISH IDENTITY

Anti-Semitism has had a unique and astounding staying power, metamorphosing from one epoch to another, one

---

For a fuller discussion of anti-Semitism and the difference between legitimate criticism of Israel and the new anti-Semitism directed against Israel, see "On Hating the Jews," *Commentary*, November 2003; "The 3Ds of Anti-Semitism," *Jerusalem Post*, February 27, 2004; and *The Case for Democracy*.

period to another, emerging in different forms to influence different civilizations in different places with different cultural lives. In each case, anti-Semitism has always been directed against that time's conception of identity, of how people defined who and what they were. When identity is religious, anti-Semitism is antireligious. When identity is national, anti-Semitism is antinational. And today, when Israel has become a vital part of Jewish identity, anti-Semitism in turn is now directed against Israel. Israel has thus become, as many have pointed out, the world's Jew: the symbol of the Jewish people and as a result the target of anti-Semitic hatred.

Many attempts have been made to explain the nature of anti-Semitism in different periods, either by trying to find specific reasons for each case and for each country or by trying to isolate some underlying reason that transcends time and space, such as the notion of Jews as a universal scapegoat. On one hand, the remarkable variety of anti-Semitism has led to denying any link between anti-Semitism's different forms. On the other hand, general explanations for it have tempted some to see the hatred against Jews as just a specific form of a more general problem, such as racism and xenophobia. According to this logic, the Holocaust is significant primarily as humanity's most destructive act of intolerance rather than as the most murderous campaign in history against the Jews. And the problem of anti-Semitism still defies a solution. In fact, it has in a sense come full circle. At the dawn of the twentieth century, Herzl thought that a Jewish state would end anti-Semitism. At the dawn of the twenty-first century, many claim that anti-Semitism will end only with the disappearance of the Jewish state.

In the face of this many-headed monster, I believe that the fullest explanation of hatred of the Jews involves not only the different forms identity takes but the question of identity itself. Jews have been repeatedly and consistently the "other" of whatever people, culture, and religion in whose midst they lived. In many places, they have been the most prominent and often the only "other," as was the case throughout most of European history and in many Muslim lands as well. In a sense, by their very exclusion, the Jews helped define European identity itself. To be Christian was to inherit and therefore displace the Jewish covenant with God. To be European was to enclose and reject the Jews as aliens in their midst. Exiling, persecuting, and killing Jews became part of European cultural history and identity; just as, in reverse form, not killing Jews and defending their rights became part of Europe's self-image of its enlightenment, emancipation, and democracy. The Napoleonic Codes, fundamental to the definition of public citizen and private person, had special reference to the Jews, who were now deemed socially acceptable as long as their religious identity remained confined to the home. In either role, Jews played a vital part in the formation of Europe, including in constructing the philosophical architecture of multicultural-ism, many of whose leading exponents are Jews. The creation of the State of Israel was seen by many in a guilt-ridden Europe as compensation for a nation whose long history of persecution had ended with the tragedy of the Holocaust. But later these feelings of guilt were transferred from Israel to the Arab world, in the context of Europe's own colonial past, with which the Zionist enterprise became mistakenly identified.

Jews have similarly played a foundational role in Islam. Like Christianity, Islam sees its Koran as replacing the Jewish Bible (and for that matter, the Christian Bible as well). As Christians saw Jews, Muslims see Jews and Christians: superseded as God's peoples, they are to be tolerated above pagans but limited to a second-class role compared to Muslims themselves. Indeed, toleration was contingent on such second-class status. The moment the Jews became a sovereign nation in their own state, Muslim toleration ended. Sovereign Jews did not fit into the narrative of the ascendancy of Islam in both this world and the next, just as for some Christians, Jewish sovereignty had not fit into the narrative of Christian inheritance of the Jewish covenant with God.

Through time, the Jews have not only been seen by non-Jews as "the other," they considered themselves to be "an other." They insisted on being different, in staying true to their identity, even if that meant standing against the current in whatever culture they found themselves. Today is no exception. Indeed, Israel stands against three currents at once.

First, Israel is an island of democracy in an ocean of tyranny. It insists on maintaining its democratic norms. Second, Israel is a Jewish state in the middle of the Muslim world. Perceived as a crusader and a colonialist state, Israel is seen by Muslims as a foreign body penetrating into the heart of Islam. And third, Israel is a nation-state that is part of a free world where post-identity is the prevailing zeitgeist. For the believers of post-identity, Israel has become equated with the colonial sins they are intent on expiating. Projecting their own history of intolerance against others, Europe vilifies Israel as a perpetrator of this intolerance. Just as Jews were "the other" for so many centuries across so many civilizations and cultures, so too today's Israel is "an other" for much of the world. In short, Israel must simultaneously defend itself on three fronts: secular dictatorships, fundamentalist Islam, and post-identity.

The first two wars can be fought, and we are fighting them, with our faith in freedom and, when necessary, with our armies. In these wars, the lines are clearly drawn. But the third war is far less clear, the lines more blurred, splitting the free world itself. This is why the war on post-identity is proving the most arduous of all.

Post-Zionism: Israeli Post-Identity

In Israel, the pied pipers of post-identity have many followers. They call themselves, not surprisingly, post-Zionists. The intellectual pedigree of post-Zionism can be traced, quite directly, to Eric Hobsbawm. The father of post-nationalism turns out to have fathered post-Zionism as well. Born in Egypt to Jewish parents, raised and educated in Vienna, Berlin, and London, he repeatedly refers to Jewish nationalism as his archetype for why nationalism is illegitimate. He put it this way in an interview:

My personal attitude is to some extent determined by my attitude towards my own particular nationalism— which would be Zionism, because I am Jewish. Zionism has been a bad development for Jews, and, consequently, I've always been opposed to it.

He continues:

I am entirely in favor of what you might call citizen patriotism, but that's a different matter. What I am opposed to is the kind of ethnic-linguistic nationalism which establishes specific identity, and especially which establishes an identity which is superior to all others. The danger of nationalism, particularly for historians, is that it eliminates the possibility of a universal discourse in which people from one background can talk to another, and argue with one another on a rational basis.

The vision of an Israel that would be secular, post-national, and post-Zionist found early formulation in the writings of Edward Said. A prominent literary critic in America, Said's highly influential book *Orientalism* is central to the modern canon of books indicting the West for its dealings with the non-West. This trailblazing work of moral relativism defines Europe and America as essentially colonialist, with other cultures their victims, and claims that it is illegitimate for the West to judge other cultures or demand or impose standards on them. Said's premises have become widely accepted not only in Mideast studies but throughout the humanities. In my numerous visits to university campuses, I could see how Said is regarded as a leading moral authority, if not prophet, among the academic left.

To Said, all the sins of the West are symbolized in the fate of the Palestinians. In recompense, Said has vigorously promoted what he calls the "One State Solution." This means the dissolution of Israel as a Jewish state into a binational one that in fact becomes indistinguishable from a wider pan-Arab world. Like Hobsbawm, Said's ultimate model is a transnational empire such as the Ottoman Empire. To Hobsbawm, "the great achievement of the communist regimes in multinational countries [was] to limit the disastrous effects of nationalism within them" (*Nations and Nationalism Since 1780*). So to Said "new and general collectivities—African, Arab, Islamic—should have precedence over particularist ones, thus setting up non-narrative connections among people whom imperialism separated into autonomous tribes, narratives, cultures" (*Culture and Imperialism*). Yet, in strong contradiction with this, Said nonetheless insists on the rights of the Palestinians to statehood and to self-determination. As he states in "The One State Solution," there will be no "withering" of Palestinian "aspirations of self-determination" because they "want at all costs to preserve their Arab identity as part of the surrounding Arab and Islamic world." For to be "Palestinian in a Jewish polity means forever chafing at inferior status." In all this discussion, there is no acknowledgment of Jewish self-determination. Apparently, according to Said, it is perfectly just for Jews to live as a minority in an Arab polity. He conceded as much in an interview he granted a few years ago to Ari Shavit, one of Israel's leading journalists:

> SHAVIT: In a binational state, the Jews will quickly become a minority, like the Lebanese Christians.

> SAID: Yes, but you're going to be a minority anyway . . . the Jews are a minority everywhere. They can certainly be a minority in Israel.

> SHAVIT: Would they be treated fairly?

> SAID: I worry about that . . . I really don't know . . .

> SHAVIT: So what you envision is a totally new situation in which a Jewish minority would live peacefully within an Arab context?

> SAID: Yes, I believe it is viable. A Jewish minority can survive the way other minorities in the Arab world survived. I hate to say it, but in a funny sort of way, it worked rather well under the Ottoman Empire, with its millet system.

> SHAVIT: So, as you see it, the Jews would eventually have a cultural autonomy within a pan-Arab structure?

> SAID: Pan-Arab or Mediterranean . . . What I would like is a kind of integration of Jews into the fabric of the

larger society, which has an extraordinary staying power despite mutilation by the nation-state. . . . My definition of pan-Arabism would comprise the other communities within an Arab-Islamic framework. Including the Jews.

SHAVIT: So, in a generation or two, what we will have is an Arab-Jewish minority community in an Arab world?

SAID: Yes. Yes. I would have thought.

To Said, who is an Arab, self-determination depends on who the self is. Minority status is fine when Jews, not Palestinians, are the minority. His post-nationalism leaves room for identities he approves of—in this case pan-Arab. Penning his invective against the West while safely ensconced at Columbia, a university situated in the financial and cultural capital of the freest country the world has ever known, Said's appeal to a supra-state model such as the Ottoman Empire favors a political structure that is far from democratic. What the Ottoman Empire offered non-Muslims was not equality but toleration as second-class citizens. This is imperialism disguised as post-nationalism. When Said speaks of a state with "shared land, equal rights for all citizens," and says that "both peoples must resolve that their existence is a secular fact," post-identity serves to mask a "pan-Arabism [that] would comprise the other communities within an Arab-Islamic framework," that is, an identity that is "Arab-Islamic," not neutral.

Said recognizes that the Palestinians began looking at themselves as a separate nation only in the last fifty years (before that they saw themselves merely as Arabs who lived in Greater Syria). But he believes that correcting world injustice requires giving the Palestinians their own state. To Siad, the same historical justice apparently demands that one of the most ancient nations on earth be denied self-determination and that they should live as a minority in their ancestral homeland in a neutral Arab-Jewish state. How can Said and his ilk explain these obvious contradictions?

To answer this question, we must return to the concept of good and bad identities. To Said, Jewish identity is bad and Palestinian identity is good. In fact, one might argue that Jewish identity is the quintessence of the bad identity. On the one hand there are bad nationalisms with "imperialist narratives of patriotic sovereignty." But on the other there are good ones that are part of "the history of all subjugated men and women." These Said calls "anti-imperialist" and "anti-authoritarian" (overlooking the fact that such movements are often authoritarian indeed). According to the peddlers of post-identity, these national movements contribute to historical progress, correcting the injustices of the past and pointing beyond "imperialist" nation-states to a post-nationalist world. These, therefore, have historic roles, while the "pro-capitalist, pro-imperialist nationalisms" are to be resisted and, if possible, eradicated.

This logic follows the precise paradigm of good and bad identities set by Marx and Engels. Even if your ultimate dream is a world without identities—as with the dream of the communist paradise—those identities that help advance the world toward this goal are seen as progressive while those that slow it down are worthy of condemnation. And judgments are subject to change. When the young Marx and Engels thought progress meant the development of capitalism and the broadening of its markets and power, France, Britain, and Germany were historical nations that had to overcome and destroy the resistance of the nonhistorical nations of Africa and Asia. When, in the next stage of the class struggle, progress required their followers to destroy capitalism (from inside), anticolonial movements were progressive and colonialism was reactionary. Similarly, for those who believe that moving to a world of post-identity represents real progress, Israel, as the last embodiment of the sin of colonialism, is a bad identity, while Palestinian nationalism, which helps to overcome that sin, is a good one.

This good identity/bad identity paradigm generates a double standard that is directed against Israel. When it comes to the good or progressive or historical or anticolonial or anti-imperialist nations, depending on how you define progress, the champions of post-identity close their eyes to cruelty. Any actions can be justified in the name of historical necessity. When it comes to bad nations, however, the very fact of their resistance to historical developments makes everything they do unjustifiable, including defending themselves against attack. Any response of theirs becomes unacceptable, because it is by definition against progress. The victims of "resistance" are barely worth mentioning. As a bad identity, Israel's basic right to exist is denied; no measure taken to defend it will be considered legitimate.

Shlomo Avineri, a political scientist who is a staunch liberal Zionist, makes this point (in the July 8, 2007, *Haaretz*), noting that post-Zionism is "fundamentally a radical criticism not just of Israel's policy; [but] at its base is a total denial of the Zionist project and of the very legitimacy of the existence of the State of Israel as a Jewish nation-state." He goes on to point out Stalinist sympathies among a radical fringe. "Even at the height of Stalin's persecution of Jews in the early 1950s, there was an active pro-Stalinist Communist movement in Israel who explained away acts of murder of Jews in Hebron and Jerusalem, committed by Palestinians in 1929, as the authentic expression of a 'popular uprising,' even if its inspiration was fanatical Islam." In the name of Marxist and Stalinist post-identity, they accepted the notion "that there is no Jewish people [as in Stalin's doctrine], that Zionism is an ally of imperialism and that the Palestinian Arabs are victims of Zionist aggression."

Although Edward Said was a major spokesman for the Palestinian cause, his arguments have been adopted by some Israelis and have been used to undermine Zionism from within. In a sense, Said is as much the inventor of post-Zionism as the spokesman for Palestinian nationhood. To Ilan Pappe, a main exponent of post-Zionism, Israel is nothing more than a "colonialist movement." Far from being "a movement to redeem a lost land after 2000 years of exile," it was "an immigration movement from Europe" that simply, apparently arbitrarily, "chose Palestine as its target territory" and then established a state "on the ruins of Palestine" (*Fifty Years through the Eyes of New Historians in Israel*). Pappe's account effectively turns Zionism on its head.

Post-Zionist ideas have not only been enormously destructive, they have gained currency. Calls for disbanding Israel altogether—as unjust and unnecessary, as colonialist and victimizing—have moved from a radical fringe into the mainstream. In a *New York Review of Books* article on October 23, 2003, that gained wide attention, Tony Judt argued that Israel is an "ethnic majority defined by language, or religion, or antiquity, or all three at the expense of inconvenient local minorities," a nation-state project in which "Jews and the Jewish religion have exclusive privileges from which non-Jewish citizens are forever excluded." According to Judt, this project has landed anachronistically in a "world that has moved on, a world of individual rights, open frontiers, and international law." He concludes, like Said, with a call for a binational state whose security "would need to be guaranteed by international force."

Here are all the telltale signs, the appeal to a paradigm that already sets up the facts to fit a foregone conclusion. Israel is an anachronistic and unjust colonizer, a bad identity in a world that has moved beyond identity into a utopia of "individual rights, open frontiers, and international law." Even if "for many years, Israel had a special meaning for the Jewish people," that time has passed, and indeed puts other Jews in danger. "Attacks on Jews in Europe and elsewhere are primarily attributable to misdirected efforts, often by young Muslims, to get back at Israel." Israel's sort of "ethno-state" therefore serves no purpose, and indeed is a threat to others in "a world where cultural and national impediments to communication have all but collapsed, where more and more of us have multiple elective identities and would feel falsely constrained if we had to answer to just one of them."

For post-identity thinkers, although strong national and religious identities are bad in principle, some identities may nonetheless temporarily contribute to the larger historical progress of defeating identity altogether. In this context, certain forms of nationalism can be good. That is why a Palestinian state is needed, whether within Said's vision of a greater pan-Arabism modeled on the Ottoman Empire or within Ilan Pappe's dream of a secular binational democratic state that replaces a Jewish one, or in Tony Judt's world of post-identity.

One might ask why anyone should pay the slightest attention to these ideologically oriented academics, however prominent they may be? After all, how much influence do they really have? The problem is that these theories are part of a broader ideology of post-identity that is increasingly dominating the thinking of the educated classes throughout the free world. When Israel insists that the world recognize its right to exist as a Jewish democratic state, and the American president does just that, few of the European countries who once backed Israel's creation and supported its right to exist all these years are ready to second him. Many attribute this reticence to a capitulation to pressure from the Arab world. But no less important to their equivocation is that the idea of a national state is unpopular today and is seen as a relic of a "reactionary past" that drags the world into war and conflict. A "democratic state of all its citizens" sounds much more progressive, much more politically correct.

In this post-identity spirit, a number of prominent political and public figures among Israel's Arab population published the Haifa Declaration in May 2007. In it, they insist that Israel as a Jewish state should be replaced by a democratic state of all its citizens, and they use the language of human rights and democracy to enlist support from the free world for erasing a Jewish state in the Middle East. Given this ambitious and increasingly potent assault from within and without on the idea of a Jewish state, the question that must be answered for anyone concerned with Israel's future is simple: Why resist? Why stand against a rising current and insist on a Jewish nation-state? There are three answers: One, because it is crucial for the survival of the Jewish people; two, because it is crucial for the free world; and three, because it is just.

Why is it crucial for Jews? The importance of Jews having the ability to defend themselves, given their experience of historic persecution, is obvious. But as important, identity is what gives meaning to our lives, what connects us with the past and with the future. Expressing a collective identity needs a collective life. The nation-state plays an important role in strengthening and deepening this feeling of identity. France launches many projects popularizing and supporting the learning of the French language in the world and no one expects it to do the same for Spanish or Arabic.

Germany, the moment the iron curtain fell, offered German citizenship to all Soviet citizens of German origin—even if their ancestors moved to Russia two hundred years ago—and no one raised the question as to why Soviet citizens of 150 other nationalities were not offered the same opportunity. That measure, along with many others like them, was viewed as a legitimate right of a national state.

Yet Israel has had to do more than simply preserve a culture. It had to secure and rebuild an imperiled national existence. Its challenge was enormous: to provide a safe haven for Jews anywhere who faced persecution, to ingather exiles scattered across the world, to resuscitate a national language that could unite a disparate people, to build a national culture, and to safeguard against assimilation. The champions of post-identity who think that the Jewish condition today obviates the need for a Jewish state are gravely mistaken.

Professor Ruth Gavison, a specialist on human rights and the former president of the Association for Human Rights in Israel, made the case this way in "The Jewish State: A Justification:"

> [W]ithout a Jewish state the Jews would revert to the status of a cultural minority everywhere. And as we know from history, the return of the Jews to minority status would likely mean the constant fear of a resurgence of anti-Semitism, persecution, and even genocide—as well as the need to dedicate ever more resources to staving off assimilation. I do not feel that I

am being overly dramatic, then, if I say that forgoing a state is, for the Jewish people, akin to national suicide.

While it is clearly important for the Jews that Israel should continue to exist as a Jewish and democratic state and not a state of all its citizens, it is also important for the world. Israel is a beachhead of freedom and democracy in a region steeped in totalitarianism and fundamentalism. It was created, and continues to function, in constant confrontation with these forces. This struggle demands from the citizens of Israel complete commitment, devotion, energy, and readiness for self-sacrifice. As we have seen, the only force potent enough to instill such a sense of commitment is the power of identity. That is why those who want to defend freedom and democracy should see it as vital that Israel maintains a strong Jewish identity. Without it, Israel will be a weaker ally for the free world in the struggle against tyranny. For the same reasons, an Israel with a strong Jewish identity will help guard the free world against its enemies. The lesson I learned in prison holds true of states: States with strong identities can make the strongest of allies.

But even if it is vital to Jewish survival that Israel be a Jewish state, and if a Jewish state contributes to the democratic world's battle against totalitarian forces, what about the principles of democracy and human rights? Isn't a democratic state of all citizens preferable to a national state?

The call for a "state for all its citizens" masks the fact that Israel, as a democracy, is already a state for all its citizens, minorities as well as the majority. More than this, every nation-state, if it is truly democratic, must be a state for all its citizens. Democracy in today's world means two inseparable parts: individual freedom and popular sovereignty. In other words, the majority decides what form society should take and how it should be governed as long as these decisions don't contradict the basic inviolable rights of individuals and the principle that all citizens are equal before the law. Ruth Gavison explains:

> Contrary to what is popularly believed, the principles of democracy, individual rights, and equality before the law do not necessitate a rejection of the Jewish character of the state. On the contrary: The fact of Israel's democratic nature means that it must also be Jewish in character, since a stable and sizable majority of its citizens wants the state to be a Jewish one.

The central question then becomes whether a national state can also be a liberal democratic state, in which equal rights for all its citizens can be guaranteed. Does Israel provide equal rights to Arabs and other minorities living in its territory?

TWO RIVAL NARRATIVES

The narrative discussed so far is a Jewish one. The Arabs have a different one, those who live inside Israel and those who live in neighboring states. Relations between Israel and the other countries of the Middle East are discussed in the context of the peace process in the next chapter. Here we address the question of Arabs who are citizens of Israel.

You will not find in the dictionaries from sixty years ago any mention of a Palestinian people. When, under the banner of modern Zionism, Jews began in larger numbers to immigrate to the Land of Israel, they found, strictly speaking, not an extant Palestinian nation but an Arab population that had been living under the rule of the Ottoman Empire and whose loyalties were local rather than national. But in the years of Arab struggle against the Jewish state, a sense of Palestinian nationhood emerged. This is true not only for those Arabs between the Jordan and Mediterranean who no longer live under Israeli rule—such as the Arab population in Gaza and those who live in Palestinian populated cities in the West Bank—but also true for the twenty percent of Israeli citizens who are Arabs (in recent years, some have begun calling themselves Palestinian-Israelis, making matters even more confusing). Regardless of how it happened, today one of the world's oldest nations and one of the world's youngest inhabit the same space: two cultures and two histories, sharing one body.

Each of these nations has its own narrative. I don't want to pretend I am an objective historian, if such a thing is even possible. Of the two narratives, Arab and Jewish, I live only one of them: the one that tells of a small group of people who, after thousands of years of exile, pogroms, persecutions, and the Holocaust, has come back to its ancient land of Israel to join the small community of Jews who had lived there since time immemorial to build a new collective identity. Our narrative unfolds against the backdrop of an indifferent world that needed the shock of an unprecedented and scarcely imaginable catastrophe to recognize the right of Jews to have their own tiny state. Only in such a state can the Jews realize their own destinies as a people in history, where their culture and religion can find not only open and secure expression but develop through sovereign collective action.

History has placed this tiny democratic state in the center of an Arab world that rejects it. And so Israel has had to fight even before it was born for its right to exist. During the struggle for its independence, hundreds of thousands of Jews, survivors from Europe and those cruelly expelled from a hostile Arab world, became citizens of Israel. During this same struggle, hundreds of thousands of Arabs living in what was then called Palestine, in the duress of war and expecting an immediate return, fled Palestine and lived in refugee camps. To keep the conflict alive, descendents of the Palestinian refugees have been kept for four generations in these refugee camps, in miserable conditions, where they can serve as a battering ram against the existence of the Jewish state.

The promises "to throw Jews into the sea," "to wipe Israel off the map," "to return to a world without Zionism" have not ceased for an instant in over sixty years, and today they are made by a fanatic Iranian regime, by its Lebanese proxy Hezbollah, and by various Palestinian terror groups, Hamas foremost among them. In 1967 Arab countries seemed perilously close to achieving their dream of destroying Israel. Israel pushed them back from the suburbs of Jerusalem and Tel Aviv and extended the borders of the Jewish state.

Yet despite the unremitting hostility toward it, Israel has consistently demonstrated its willingness to make painful compromises for the sake of peace, as long as these concessions left the State of Israel viable and defensible. But while Israel has signed peace agreements with Egypt and Jordan, peace has not come. Palestinian leaders, supported directly or indirectly by many Arab leaders, have insisted that the existence of Israel is an injustice that must be righted. For them, the conflict is not territorial but existential. It will not be solved by establishing a state alongside Israel but rather by establishing a state instead of Israel. That is why every concession made by Israel turns into an additional weapon for terror against it and why new generations of Palestinians are indoctrinated to reject Israel and to do anything to destroy it.

The Arab narrative is fundamentally different. It tells of displacement and occupation: of a cruel and colonial Zionist regime that is the last colonization project of Europe, where Arabs have been made to pay for the sins of Nazis. The events of 1948 are a *nakba*, or catastrophe, that was inflicted on the Arab world when this state, hostile to their faith and tradition, an infidel and decadent democratic intrusion of the West, was imposed on them and founded in the very midst of their historic Islamic world. According to this view, Palestinians were brutally driven from their homes as part of a deliberate program of mass ethnic cleansing, and four generations of Palestinians are still paying for this crime by living in the dire conditions of refugee camps in Palestine, Jordan, and Lebanon. But the hope of the refugees never dies. They keep the keys from the houses of their grandfathers in Haifa, Lod, and Jerusalem under their pillows, and they know and believe that the day will come when justice will be restored; that they will return to their forefathers' homes.

Not everyone accepts one or the other of the narratives absolutely. There are Israelis who are post-Zionists and embrace the Arab narrative; while many, if not most Druze, share the Israeli narrative. But these two bold outlines govern what remain two irreconcilable understandings of the past and the future. They reflect a deep conflict between two strong identities.

How can a democratic state function in which two different populations have such absolutely incompatible narratives—narratives that have become part of the culture, historical memory, and identity of each people and that in many ways define who they are? In a democratic state, what should be the relation between the majority and minority cultures of peoples who cannot be turned, by any decree, into one people? These are questions Israel must answer. For a critical test of Israel's democratic character and indeed of its legitimacy is whether it is committed and able to protect the right of the Arab minority to express its identity.

Although the two narratives can never be fully reconciled, certainly not with regard to history, they can be accommodated within the norms of a democratic state such as Israel. Democracy requires that any minority have the rights possessed by the majority—their rights to express themselves as individuals and their rights to express themselves as part of a group; the right to embrace a particular cultural life and to strengthen their own unique identity. Of course, the practical implementation of this is not always simple. When I was a minister responsible for making difficult decisions to solve practical problems—in housing, in industry, in municipal life—I constantly confronted challenges that were as complicated logistically as they were ideologically. It is not easy to create equivalent economic conditions between an Arab village with infrastructure from the eighteenth century and an Israeli community established thirty years ago. Political fears and prejudices turn every decision into a potentially dramatic conflict.

In 2000, I became the first Israeli minister of interior who decided to transfer territory under the control of a Jewish town into the municipal jurisdiction of an Arab village, in response to the village's wish to build its own industrial zone. This decision was straightforward in terms of basic common sense, but it was exceedingly difficult nonetheless because of the highly charged ideological struggle. Quite a few people criticized this decision or had misgivings about it. But this is perhaps inevitable in the building of Israel's democratic state. A long and arduous process is required to overcome the historic gap in development; an even longer and more arduous one is needed to overcome the historic gap in trust. But despite the difficulties and the chasms that remain between Jews and Arabs, Israel has much in which it can take pride. The Arab minority of Israel has the highest standard of living, the highest level of education, and the lowest death rate and mortality rate for children of any comparable population in the Arab world. Similarly, Arab parliamentarians in the Knesset have a freedom to criticize their own government that they do not have in any other parliament of the Arab world.

It is not surprising then that Israeli-Arabs are adamantly opposed to giving up their Israeli citizenship. In fact, a huge number of Palestinians try to obtain Israeli citizenship. As minister of interior (the person in Israel who deals with citizenship issues), I was exposed to thousands and thousands of Palestinians who wanted to become citizens of Israel. Yet I did not hear of a single case where a citizen of Israel wanted to become a citizen of any other Arab country. More than a third and perhaps as many as half of Israeli-Arabs vote for Zionist parties. Nearly forty-five percent of Israeli-Arabs consider themselves Israeli patriots. Both my positive experiences working together with many Israeli-Arab leaders on the improvement of the lives of their fellow Arabs as well as my negative experiences fighting against a radical minority who are trying to circumvent the law convince me that the overwhelming majority of Israeli-Arabs desire to be loyal citizens. As I write this I am aware that many of my friends will accuse me of naïve idealism, because the voices of extremists among Israeli-Arabs have become louder and some of them have become much more violent. I believe that this is a direct result of the fact that the extremists, whether under Hezbollah, Hamas, or Iranian

leadership, have become stronger and stronger. The antagonistic attitude of Israeli-Arabs toward Israel is encouraged
each time Israeli democracy looks weak and when there is a
growing sense that Israel as a Jewish state is a passing
episode. In such an environment, extremists sooner or later
will gain strength and challenge both Israel's Jewish identity
and its democracy.

An instructive experience for me of how dangerous it is
to make concessions to extremists, to follow the path of
appeasement, occurred in the case of the Church of the
Annunciation in Nazareth. Nazareth is the third most
important site for Christians in the Holy Land. In 1997, the
municipality of Nazareth decided to renovate the square
around the church to create a large center for tourists from
all over the world. In the days before the project was to be
launched, a group of extremists from a newly born fundamentalist Islamic movement occupied the square, declaring
they would not allow the tourist site to be built and
demanding that a mosque be built on the square to com-
memorate the grave of one of their local sheiks. The police
could have launched an operation that very day to remove
the couple of hundred hooligans from the square. But anx-
ious and intimidated, fearing that the issue was too sensitive,
the government decided to negotiate with this small group of
extremists. They even proposed a compromise: They would
allow them to build a small mosque on the site. Not surprisingly, appeasement did not lead to a solution. It instead
turned the small group of extremists into a rising and, over
time, powerful movement. The square was not evacuated.

For the next five years the Islamist movement kept the square under its control, turning it into a de facto mosque, a place for prayers and meetings, and their demands constantly increased. In the end, they insisted on building the tallest and largest mosque in the Middle East, which would have cast a shadow on the Church of the Annunciation.

As this Nazareth tale was unfolding, the Islamist movement gained strength and a wider following, until it felt strong enough to call for and begin a project for building a new mosque on the Temple Mount itself. They excavated and built another underground floor and turned it into an additional floor for the mosque in place of Solomon's Stables. (These excavations have been viewed by many archeologists as one of the major cases of archeological destruction in modern history.) The Israeli government was afraid to intervene, which further encouraged and strengthened the popularity of the extremists among other Arabs. The crisis deepened due to Israeli inaction and began to involve more of the Muslim world. Afraid to complicate relations with this growing circle of interested parties, government after government in Israel continued to look for new and more far-reaching compromises.

The free world was more or less indifferent to the archeological destructions on the Temple Mount. But when Moslem extremists started to build their giant mosque in Nazareth, the Christian world began to protest. As a result, Prime Minister Sharon—the third prime minister to deal with this problem—created a new government commission to study the situation and prepare a new proposal for the government to consider. As the then minister of housing and a deputy prime minister, I was asked to head the commission.

I called for an open public review of the entire situation. Historians, sociologists, and political and religious leaders of different faiths participated. These open hearings were to include representatives from the Vatican and other Christian churches, as well as religious public and political Arab figures. While the Christian representatives passionately called for an immediate stop to the abuse of a sacred site, the message from at least some of the Arab religious leaders and Arab members of the Knesset was threatening. I was told in no uncertain terms that any attempt to deny them the right to build the mosque would trigger a bloodbath across the Mideast. I was warned that there would be pogroms against Jews everywhere in the Moslem world, in outrage that Jews would take sides in a conflict between Muslims and Christians.

Then came the final chapter in this episode that took me by surprise. We went to Nazareth to hold local hearings. Lawyers, businessmen, an editor of the local newspaper, and influential members of the community, both Arab Moslems and Christians, asked to talk to me face to face, in private, without protocols, to deliver a message. It would be a tragedy, each of them said privately, to give in to the extremists. The city already had begun to live in an atmosphere of fear. Only by opposing extremist demands and taking a stand against them could we rescue the community. The respected members of the community had become afraid to speak publicly. But they wanted the state to act. I realized that our appeasement had betrayed not only Christian identity, not only moderate Moslems, but democracy itself.

I understood then that even in the midst of a democratic country, a culture of fear can take root. I understood how permitting extremists to command and intimidate could undermine freedom even within a society pledged to defend it.

It became clear to me that we had to take a stand. We proposed three sites nearby on which to build a mosque of whatever size the Muslims wanted. This, however, did not satisfy the extremists. The truth is that their demand was not about building a mosque but about the struggle to establish their leadership role in the Muslim community and to bid for control over the city. Accordingly, we decided we had to act to clear the square. The Shabak (Israel's FBI) was supportive but the police were scared. They feared bloodshed, riots, protests, attacks. Nevertheless, I decided to propose to the government that the square be evacuated, the tourist center built, and a mosque built on a nearby site if the Muslim community wanted it.

To minimize the danger of bloodshed in taking this decision, I wanted to build a coalition. All those who wanted our help had to be willing to support our decision. Here we ran into difficulties. The representatives of the Vatican in Israel urged us to act. But what about the Pope? Would the church be ready to support us publicly? I happened to be traveling to New York, and I set up a meeting with the Cardinal there to ask him to help enlist the Pope's support. When we met, he was familiar with the situation. I told him: "Representatives of the Church have asked us to intervene.

Muslim extremists are threatening massive violence against Jews. This is a very difficult situation for us. We have come to the conclusion that we should protect the Church but there are threats of pogroms, bloodbaths, and international denunciations of Israel. The Catholic Church has enormous worldwide influence. We ask for your support for our decision, not least to help prevent this decision from arousing public opinion against Israel."

The Cardinal replied that Israel should protect the Church. But he added, "I hear from the Catholic street that there are many who believe the whole incident is a Jewish provocation from the start. Therefore we cannot interfere or publicly support you." The one reply I could summon was "this report from your street that Jews are the problem is something we have heard for the last two thousand years."

When the government was debating my proposal, thousands of policemen were brought to the area to prevent the riots that were predicted if the decision were implemented. But they were not needed. All the warnings and threats turned out to be a bluff. There was no bloodbath and no violence. The moment the government started to act, the Islamic movement lost its power and attraction in Nazareth, which quickly returned to being a democratic city in which people were not afraid to speak.

The lesson for democratic society is simple: appeasement never works. It only strengthens the position of extremists and their commitment to their extremism. It creates within a democratic society people controlled by fear.

In Israel, a policy of support and cooperation with local Arab leaders is possible and necessary. We must work with those who support Israeli democracy, while standing firmly against those who oppose it and threaten it. This is the only way to secure mutual coexistence with Arabs in Israel.

Each time the idea of a Jewish state is undermined, extremists are emboldened. No doubt the post-Zionist idea of replacing the Jewish state with a "state of all citizens" has given great encouragement to those who are not willing to accept Israel's existence, even as they also themselves reject the democracy they are appealing to. The form of the recent Haifa Declaration, calling for the removal of all Jewish settlements and the Right of Return as a disguised call for a Jewish minority in an Arab state, is a direct result of the success of this post-Zionist ideology. For those of us who remain committed to both Jewish identity and democracy, this unfortunately strengthens the fear that Arabs are the main danger for our state. But I am sure everything depends on us.

Israel can maintain a robust democracy in which strong identities can flourish. For Jews, this inevitably means identities linked through a shared history, a shared destiny, and the collective reality of daily life in Israel. For Arabs, it is up to them to choose to what extent they want to become integrated into the culture and history of the developing Israeli state, or whether they want to remain autonomous communities, linked to the state only through a respect for the democratic laws and norms that make this choice possible.

Not only can Israel remain a Jewish and democratic state. Its survival depends on it.

CHAPTER 8

Peace or War

NO WORD IS MORE USED, and more abused, than the word *peace*—even more than the word *democracy*. For the sake of peace, everything can be done. In the USSR, all public life was devoted to the "struggle for peace." When the Soviet Union changed its orthography to replace the old Tsarist one, the words *peace* and *world* came to be written the same way—*mir.* The ubiquitous slogan during my childhood was "Miru Mir," peace to the world. This helped only to emphasize how peaceful were the attempts of the Soviet Union to extend its power worldwide. All progressive mankind belonged to the peace camp. The Red Army, which controlled one third of the globe, was called the Army of Peace. In the name of the victory of peace, dissidents were sent to prison, missiles were sent to Cuba, and tanks were sent to Prague.

But the word *peace* is loved not only by dictators. When Chamberlain came back from Munich in 1939, where he served Czechoslovakia's Sudetenland as an appetizer to Hitler, he infamously declared at the airport that he had brought "peace in our time." And today, in our post-communist world, uses of the word *peace* know few limits. When I was working at the *Jerusalem Report* at the beginning of the 1990s, an editor kept calling one of the leaders of the PLO a "peace activist." This was before Oslo, when the PLO was legally considered a terrorist organization and openly committed to terrorism. So I asked for the explanation as to why we were giving such a title to a person who refused even to recognize the right of Israel to exist. The editor's answer was that unlike his PLO colleagues, this "peace activist" wanted to destroy Israel by peaceful means.

Of course, one reason for the ubiquity of the word *peace* is that the concept is dear to all of us. The peace camp includes the overwhelming majority of mankind. It includes all those who hope that their children will not have to risk their lives in wars and all those who do not want to live in constant fear for themselves and for their children.

In this sense, peace becomes something of a synonym for life. Life itself is understandably regarded as the highest human value. Yet in truth, for the majority of people, peace (or life) is not really the highest value. It depends what type of peace (or life) one is talking about. Those English who so warmly greeted Chamberlain's statement about bringing peace found themselves later risking their lives fighting at the front. By then, they, and the rest of Britain, preferred to fight and die in a war for liberty than live under a peaceful German dictatorship.

No Peace without Identity

In *Faust*, Goethe said: "Only those who every day fight for life and freedom deserve it." Goethe links life directly with freedom—it is as if the two aspects were part of a single entity. For life to be valued it must be free; the life of a slave is not a life fully lived. Freedom, not peace, liberates life. Every person, group, community, and nation can formulate for themselves the values that give life meaning, the values for which they are ready to fight and if necessary die, the things for which they are even willing to sacrifice peace.

To live freely is to be able to live according to the things you value most, to play whatever part you want in your culture and history, to draw from your chosen traditions, and to pass them on through your own manifestation of them. In short, to live freely is to be able to express, and live according to your identity. To maintain this type of life the Pentecostals in the Soviet Union retreated deeper and deeper into Siberia and were willing to be imprisoned to teach their children their religion. For the freedom to practice their religion and pursue their way of life, the Puritans left England to go to America. Because identity is so powerful, resistance to a country that threatens a particular culture or religion or way of life is always the strongest and fiercest.

For this reason identity in the West is seen today by many as a potential cause of war and the enemy of peace. For some, the very fact that people are ready to die for it turns the idea of identity into an enemy of peace. This attitude creates a seemingly irresolvable paradox: The ultimate objective of a peaceful world is for people to be able to express their identities, yet the expression of identity gives rise to conflict and erodes peace. However, identity is not the enemy of peace and the cause for war, but is the *suppression* of identity. This was John Locke's insight in his famous and groundbreaking "A Letter Concerning Toleration," penned as a response to the religious wars of the sixteenth and seventeenth centuries, which were the most enduring and cruel that Europe had ever seen. In his letter, Locke showed how, contrary to the conventional statecraft of Europe that was based on the idea that public order required all people to share one religion, it was the attempt to impose one religion that was in fact the cause of public disorder, conflict, and war.

Three centuries later, a statecraft that considers meaningful differences of identity a threat to peace is once again the dominant view. In the free world, peace is seen as the outgrowth of a weakening of the influence of identity on the life of the individual and society. To live in peace is in essence to overcome differences of identity by erasing those differences. This is the philosophy of post-identity. Transcending identity, because it helps erase differences, is seen as a force leading to peace and harmony. Democracy is seen as inherently opposed to identity, at best tolerating it, at worst threatened by it.

But this view ignores the deepest feelings and the most familiar frameworks of most human beings. It ignores the desire to preserve one's own way of life, to pass on the values and traditions we have ourselves inherited, the things that give meaning to life beyond the material self. By weakening identity, the readiness of society to fight for itself and to defend itself is weakened. A society that abandons identity sheds its protective armor, making it an inviting target for tyrants and terrorists who seek to extend their power. Post-identity weakens identity to decrease tensions between people, but doing so leads to vulnerability, threats, blackmail, and ultimately to an inability to defend against aggression. That is why post-identity is an invitation to war.

There is a famous story of Napoleon, who, when he came into a small Jewish *shtetl* in Eastern Europe, saw how the people were crying on the ninth of Av. When he asked why, he was told that three thousand years before, the Temple had been destroyed on that day. He is said to have answered: A people who still weeps over the destruction of their culture three thousand years ago will endure forever.

The opposite is true as well. If the Jews' strong identity ensured their survival, the collapse of that identity would spell their demise. Speaking to an Israeli journalist about the time he spent in prison, a Palestinian terrorist describes the moment when he was convinced that Israel would be destroyed. After seeing a prison guard eating bread on Passover, he asked why he was not observing Jewish tradition. The guard replied: "I feel no obligation to events that took place over 2000 years ago. I have no connection to that." By his own account, that was the moment when the terrorist believed that the Palestinians could achieve all their goals. He determined to "fight for everything—not a percentage, no such crumbs as the Israelis might throw us—but for everything. Because opposing us is a nation that has no connection to its roots, which are no longer of interest to it." Unfortunately, this was not understood by peacemakers devoted to solving the Israeli-Arab conflict.

PEACE PROCESS OR WAR PROCESS?

Removing identities is neither possible nor desirable, nor will it bring peace. Yet this was the central strategy of the Oslo peace process as envisaged by the West and even by Israel itself.

It is generally believed that the real peace process between the State of Israel and the Palestinians started in 1993 with the signing of the agreements reached in Oslo. Technically the basis of these agreements was the understanding that Israel would recognize the PLO, an organization that had since its inception preached and practiced terror against Jews and against Arab states willing to accept the existence of Israel. According to the agreement, Israel would transfer to the PLO, in stages, control over the lives of Palestinians in Gaza and the West Bank (captured in 1967) as well as territories in which they lived. The PLO in turn would cease all hostile activity against Israel and gradually become the leaders of a country that would live together with Israel in peace.

What did the Oslo Accords mean from the point of view of the balance between democracy and identity in the Mideast? From the beginning of the Oslo process, the question of the development and encouragement of democracy in Palestinian society was ignored. Yasser Arafat was seen as a stabilizing leader not because he was a democrat but because he was a dictator. Strengthening Arafat by all means became the top priority, even if it meant transferring public money into Arafat's private accounts, destroying the beginnings of a free economy, and refusing to support real democratic dissidents among Palestinians. As a result, with the active assistance of the free world, one of the most corrupt and primitive dictatorships in the world emerged, which became the enemy of Israel, of peace, and of its own Palestinian citizens as well.

Another important illusion that accompanied the Oslo process had to do with the question of Israel's identity. It is baffling that a strong, independent Jewish state, which had to pay such a heavy price for its right to exist, fighting from the first moment of its birth, could agree to sign a treaty with a terrorist organization committed to its destruction without demanding from the PLO the recognition of the right of Israel to exist as a Jewish state. Ari Shavit, a respected journalist from the Israeli Left, called Oslo a "colossal mistake" in its "decision to recognize the Palestinian-Arab people, its legitimate rights in this land and its national movement, without obtaining recognition of the parallel rights of the Jewish-Israeli people in return."

It is difficult to understand how such serious, fateful

decisions, which opened the way to the creation of a dictatorial Palestinian state that reaches to the very suburbs of Jerusalem, Tel Aviv, and other major Israeli cities, were taken without any serious discussion of Israel's defense needs, the potential effect on its economy and resources, and above all, on its identity. The explanation for this colossal oversight can be found in the ideology of the architects of Oslo, clearly presented in many speeches and articles and perhaps most prominently in the book by its chief architect, Shimon Peres, entitled *The New Middle East,* in which the then foreign minister laid out his vision for the region.

Peres was one of the closest assistants to Ben-Gurion and played a unique part in the creation and building of the Israeli state, particularly in helping the state develop the means to defend itself. But as he asserts again and again in his book, the time of particular nationalism has come and gone. After the failure of communism, Peres writes, the world had "moved beyond ideological confrontations. . . . The movements of the Jewish national renaissance and the Arab national renaissance met and clashed. But the world in which these two movements grew to fruition no longer exists."

Peres argued that in a world of ballistic missiles and weapons of mass destruction, territory and defensible borders play no role and have no meaning. He explained that no country in the Middle East can guarantee its security by itself. According to Peres, only regional cooperation between countries can guarantee peace. The same, he argued, is true about economic cooperation. Just as Europe once united its efforts because it had a common enemy in Stalinist communism, Peres's New Middle East would unite against a common enemy as well—poverty. As was true for the EU, "global economic interdependence of countries will bring to solidarity." But this regional cooperation would become possible only after the Arab-Israeli conflict was solved. It can be and would be solved because the leaders of both sides had to understand that no military victory could solve their problem. Peace treaties signed by the leaders with the support of the global financial powers would bring peace, prosperity, and welfare to the Middle East, exactly as they had to Europe. This time it would not be national states but post-national structures that would be the guarantors of stability and peace. "At the threshold of the twenty-first century we do not need to enforce sovereignty but rather to strengthen the position of humankind."

Shimon Peres in his free time is known to write poetry. Even his political speeches are very poetic. Probably he is the most visionary poet among all politicians and the most important poet of post-nationalism. The Oslo Accords became the first post-national international treaty, built on the idea that borders and territories are not important for defense, peace, and prosperity.

With the Oslo Accords, post-Zionism, which was already influential among Israeli intellectuals, rushed into the world of politics and down the corridors of a state now standing open to it. Peres had written: "particularist nationalism is fading and the idea of citizen of the world is taking hold." The goal of weakening national particularism, in the name of being a citizen of the world and to accelerate the peace process begun at Oslo, started influencing practically all aspects of Israeli official policy.

A few months before Oslo, the Foreign Ministry closed its Information Department, which meant it stopped fighting on the international scene for recognition of the Israeli narrative. I asked then Deputy Foreign Minister Yossi Beilin: How are we going to defend Israel, not with military weapons but with the weapons of ideas? His answer was: If we are serious in our movement towards peace, the world will understand and support us. If not, no propaganda will help us.

Ten years later, traveling all over the world to universities, so often the centers of anti-Israel propaganda in America and Europe, I heard again and again nostalgic remarks from our diplomats about the different programs that Israel used to have, which had all been suspended just when the war of ideas was becoming the central battle.

In the meantime, the Education Ministry was preparing a new program that gave special emphasis to universal values as opposed to Jewish ones. The new ethics code of the army eliminated all words such as Zionism and downplayed any connection to the Diaspora or to the building of a Jewish state. For many years, trips of Israeli youth to the World War II death camps in Poland were seen as helping to strengthen their tie to and understanding of Jewish history, and the importance of the existence of the State of Israel. But in the post-identity atmosphere of Oslo, these trips were frowned upon. The then minister of education, Shulamit Aloni, after traveling with a group of youth to Auschwitz, spoke against the continuation of these trips, arguing that they stirred up nationalist sentiment among the youth.

Many of the youngsters who went on these trips took with them Israeli flags, and wrapped themselves in them during the most dramatic or difficult moments of their journey into this horrific past. I know from my own daughters, who went on these trips, how important they felt the flag to be, to feel themselves protected by Israeli identity: both for security and to assert powerfully the fact of continuing Jewish life. Approaching one of these schoolchildren wearing such a flag, Aloni demanded to know why the student needed it: "Isn't it enough to be a good human being to protest against all this?" As she said later "What is important is that they come back from these trips better human beings, not better Jews."

The so-called Oslo peace process took place between two societies moving in directly opposite directions in terms of identity. Israeli society was being pushed in the direction of cosmopolitanism. Palestinians, under Arafat's corrupt dictatorship, were going through a crash course in hatred of Jews, Israel, and Zionism and making the rejection of Jewish-Israeli identity the basis of their own. *The hope for peace became predicated on a rejection of Israeli identity and a rejection of Palestinian democracy.* On one side stood democracy without identity. On the other stood identity without democracy. The explosion was inevitable.

The peace process soon became a war process and has remained a war process ever since. Palestinian civil society was dismantled; Palestinian hatred toward Israel has grown;

Israeli identity has been undermined. No meaningful peace process is currently underway in the Middle East.

WEAKENING IDENTITY

I have twice resigned from Israeli governments. In both cases I felt that our readiness for concessions for the sake of peace instead endangered both peace and our own security.

The first time was when Ehud Barak, in his negotiations with Arafat, offered more and more concessions to the Palestinians, including a pledge to divide Jerusalem. He was ready to give to Yasser Arafat everything he thought was important to Arafat: the Muslim Quarter, the Christian Quarter, and the Temple Mount, and special arrangements would be made for Jews to be bussed to the Western Wall. To Barak, these concessions were a price worth paying for a peace agreement. He even thought of a deal whereby everything on the surface of the Temple Mount would belong to the Palestinians and everything under the surface would belong to the Jews. It was as if he felt that our identity belonged only to an archaeological museum, not to our present and future. Barak explained his logic to me, hoping to convince me to stay in the government and even to go with him to Camp David. Natan, he said, if Arafat accepts this proposal, then however painful these concessions are, we will have peace and that is the most precious thing we wish for. But if Arafat refuses such a generous offer, he continued, the sympathies of all the world will be with us and no one will have any doubts as to the justice of our position and our struggle.

After numerous attempts to convince Barak against offering everything we were fighting for—our existence as a culture and people, religion, and history—I refused to go to Camp David and I resigned. There is no chance, I warned my prime minister, that your sacrificing our identity for the sake of peace will deliver peace from Camp David. When we are demonstrating such extreme weakness and fear, wanting peace at any price, the response can only be war.

While Barak was trying to convince himself and all of us that peace was more important than identity, Arafat demonstrated that he understood the importance of a connection of a people to their history and culture. At the very moment when Barak was offering Jerusalem to Arafat, Arafat was insisting to the entire world that a Jewish temple never existed on the Temple Mount. While Barak was busy in the name of peace trying to give away our present and future, Arafat was busy trying to take away our past.

During the time I was sitting in a tent protesting Barak's plan to divide Jerusalem, I heard on the radio Arafat saying that Jerusalem was "our heart and our blood," that he would "never make any concessions about Jerusalem without consulting first with the Muslim nations." Arafat insisted that Jerusalem belonged to all Muslims. But Barak was acting as if it did not have any meaning for Jewish people at large, not even the majority of Israeli-Jews. That evening Ehud Barak called me from Camp David. I quoted Arafat to him and said: "You do not have the support of the people of Israel, yet you dare propose to give up on Jerusalem, the heart of our identity?"

The indifference to identity by the architects of the peace process was glaringly apparent in a brief conversation I had that year at one of the government meetings with then Minister of Justice Yossi Beilin. He was explaining to me that if we gave the Moslem and Christian Quarters of Jerusalem to Arafat, there was a good chance we could have a deal with him. I objected, stating that this contradicted what Arafat himself was saying—that Arafat was demanding much more than this, not just the Muslim and Christian Quarters but also the Temple Mount and beyond. But I said to Beilin: Put aside the Moslem Quarter for the moment—why give to them the Christian Quarter and its holy places, which includes Golgotha, the Church of the Holy Sepulcher? Does Arafat have more right to the Christian Quarter than we do? Will he protect freedom of worship for Christians better than Israel has? Every place that had come under the control of Arafat had quickly been Islamicized. In Bethlehem, for the first time in centuries, there were fewer Christians than Muslims.

Beilin looked at me in sincere surprise. If he wants it, let him have it, he said. Why should we care about giving the Palestinians control of the Christian Quarter to obtain peace? I answered: Arafat knows why. If he controls the Christian Quarter, he controls the most sacred places in the world for one billion Christians, an influence he will use not for strengthening peace but against Israel. Beilin seemed simply not to understand what I was talking about. I suppose that when you do not appreciate the power of your own identity, you cannot be expected to appreciate the power of identity for hundreds of millions of others across the globe.

Under Barak's leadership, an absurd situation developed. For Arafat and his supporters, nothing was more important than Jerusalem. For Israeli leaders, Jerusalem became a bargaining chip to be used for peace—a peace that would deny the Jewish attachment to Jerusalem! I felt that this impression had to change as soon as possible. In the end, it was my wife, Avital, who came up with the idea of the biggest demonstration in the history of Jerusalem. According to police estimates, four hundred thousand people gathered around the walls of the Old City to swear an oath to Jerusalem. Usually it takes months to plan such a large demonstration. This time it took less than a week. It seemed that Jews in Israel were more than willing to declare: Without Jerusalem there can be no peace.

At this demonstration I received a bonus. It was the only time I ever had the opportunity to listen to my wife speak before a large group of people. I had heard from many people, all over the world, about the strong impression Avital had made in her speeches during my years in a Soviet prison. But after I was released, Avital, it seemed, decided I could take over this job. She was reluctant to give speeches. At the Jerusalem demonstration, she recalled how at my Moscow trial my final words had been: "Next year in Jerusalem." She continued: "Jerusalem defended us in Russia. Now it is time for us to defend Jerusalem." The crowd was clearly moved by Avital's words and by their circumstances—the walls of the Old City that had observed thousands of years of Jewish history seemed to lend the force of their support to the huge crowd. Throughout the world, and especially in Washington, it became clear that Barak did not speak for the Jewish people, nor did he have a mandate to divide Jerusalem.

True to form, despite all the concessions he was offered at Camp David, Arafat turned Barak down. In truth, no concessions would have been enough to satisfy Arafat. Once identity is on the bargaining table, the other party expects a total surrender. Soon after, Arafat launched the second Intifada. Waves of suicide bombings swept Israeli cities and, despite Barak's prediction, the world was just as hesitant to back Israel's struggle as it had been before.

I resigned from the government for the second time five years later, when Ariel Sharon was prime minister, because I disagreed with his policy of the evacuation of Jewish communities in Gaza. In my letter of resignation, I argued that this enormous, one-sided concession would not make the situation better for Israel, for the Palestinians, or for the chance to build a democratic society in the Middle East. The only beneficiaries would be Hamas, a pan-Islamist fundamentalist group who would turn Gaza into the biggest base of terror in the region. Unfortunately, within months my dire predictions had become true.

Sharon, unlike Barak, was not trying to appease the Palestinians with concessions, thinking these would cease their attacks. He explained to me: The Arabs are not going to accept the fact of our existence. Only our strong army will protect us from them. Our real problem is that the free world is pressing us for more and more concessions. They pushed for the Road Map, but even though the Palestinians are not fulfilling its requirements they already demand from us further concessions. I want to break this vicious circle. I want to make very painful concessions, after which nobody will demand from us anything more. It will be clear to all that now the ball is in the Palestinian court, that it is for them to do what is necessary if there is to be peace. I don't believe the Palestinians will give us this peace, but I want ten years without pressure on us from the free world. During these ten years we will build our state, reinforce our security, and strengthen our economy.

In effect, Ariel Sharon's intention was to appease not the Palestinians but the free world. He thought that dramatic concessions would stop the constant criticism of Israel. The concessions he proposed and then carried out were enormous. Israel did not only simply withdraw from territory. The Israeli army destroyed twenty Jewish settlements and removed every Jew who had lived there. Israel was accepting the fact that any territory under Palestinian rule would be *Judenrein*, emptied of Jews.

The response to Barak's offers to Arafat's dictatorship was the second Intifada. The consequence of Sharon's disengagement from Gaza was a Hamas Islamist dictatorship, the Second Lebanon War, the launching of thousands of rockets within the pre-1967 borders, and the further erosion of Israel's legitimacy throughout the world. In both cases the path of appeasement through concessions failed to bring peace.

Sharon's hopes of appeasing Europe and stopping the pressure of the free world were as hopeless and baseless as Barak's hopes of appeasing Arafat. The appeasement of terrorists cannot succeed in bringing peace because their aim is the destruction of Israel as a Jewish state, and nothing less than its disappearance will satisfy them. And it is impossible to appease ideologies of post-nationalism because to them the core problem is the identity of the Jewish state—an identity without which Israel, and the very purposes for which it was established, will cease to exist.

For Muslim fundamentalists, Israel is a hostile identity, and as long as Israel exists, their aim is not fulfilled. For post-nationalists, Israel is a colonial identity that, in the words of Emanuele Ottolenghi, is "the embodiment of the demons of [Europe's] own past." And as long as Israel exists as a Jewish state, they will see the struggle of the Palestinians against Israel as justified or at least understandable.

In trying to weaken its own Jewish identity in the name of post-nationalism, Israel is attempting, on the world stage, to do what some Jews have done throughout the ages: to give up their own identity in order to be accepted by the societies in which they lived. In general, Jews took one of two routes. They would weaken either their own identity or the identity of society around them. The former led to calls for assimilation. The latter led to participation in ideological movements committed to creating totally new identities, movements that promised to fundamentally change the relations of members of society on the basis of new criteria. These are the "isms" that modern times have seen so much of: Marxism, communism, and now post-nationalism. The idea of these "isms" was basically the same: to remove all previous identities in the name of some universal principle that will overcome differences.

History proves that attempts to weaken identity did not help Jews avoid the persecutions of anti-Semitism. It did not bring peace. The readiness of the Jewish state to thin its Jewish identity in order to be accepted by the global community will not buy peace, for itself or for the region or for the world. Fundamentalist Islam seeks to wipe out Jewish identity and absorb Israel into a monolithic Muslim rule, headed by a caliphate. European post-nationalism rejects the separateness of Jewish identity and imagines a democratic order without identity that will pacify the region.

Peace will not be achieved by giving up on Jewish identity. Such concessions deny the importance of identity, which gives a society both purpose and resolve. They capitulate to the demands of those who seek to destroy identity. Democracies that are ready to compromise identity for the sake of peace not only weaken their inner strength but encourage in totalitarian forces around them the belief that they can overcome societies that have cut off their roots, have disconnected themselves from their histories, and are prepared to watch their values and the qualities that give their lives meaning wither and die.

There is another way. The path to peace lies in strengthening Israel's Jewish identity, maintaining a robust Israeli democracy, and encouraging our non-democratic neighbors to build free societies.

CONCLUSION

Building a New Alliance

IN THIS BOOK I have tried to show why identity and freedom can and must be allies in a common struggle. Unfortunately this alliance is under constant assault, while a dangerous alliance is strengthening every day. It should be obvious that waging a struggle against totalitarian forces first requires moral clarity. Unless you recognize evil, you cannot begin to fight it. But this is where the champions of post-identity have done the greatest damage. When a coalition can be forged between well-intentioned liberals and the most antidemocratic forces on the planet, moral confusion rules the day.

Nowhere is the morally confused coalition more prominent than on university campuses in Europe and in America.

During my visits to Western universities—in the last few years I have spoken at more than forty of them, thirty in the United States—I saw many cases of cooperation between totalitarian forces and naïve idealists. One particularly memorable moment for me was my visit to Rutgers University. At a time when a wave of suicide bombings was engulfing Israel and claiming hundreds of victims, including personal friends, neighbors and colleagues, anti-Israeli forces were organizing at Rutgers their largest national rally in solidarity for the struggle against Zionism. Some liberal professors joined with anti-Zionist groups to oppose my speaking at the university. When I arrived, awaiting me at the entrance to the hall was a colorful demonstration. There were Arab youths wearing *kaffiahs,* raising their hands in victorious fists, as if they were mimicking video tapes of young suicide bombers giving their last interviews. They were standing shoulder to shoulder with liberal students and shouting slogans, with signs reading "Racist Israel" and "War Criminals" and "Stop the Israeli Genocide." In this theater of the absurd, students espousing the supreme importance of human rights stood together with sympathizers of suicide bombings in a carnival of hatred.

In the hall itself a small group of young Muslim women had captured the strategic position in the first rows. As a rule these were the groups who prepared the most difficult questions, with the most awful stories of Israeli atrocities. In different parts of the hall I could hear debates between pro- and anti-Israeli students. My Israeli bodyguard had not received additional support from the local authorities. He was alone and he told me: "The atmosphere is very tense. Go straight to the center of the stage. Don't stand in the crowd. It will be difficult for me to protect you from all directions simultaneously." But I dismissed this proposal. After all, direct dialogue was one of the main aims of my visit.

But the dialogue was a little too direct. I had just taken a chair in the first row and begun to answer the questions from students when all of a sudden a young boy, who I later learned headed the student group Jews against Occupation, shouted "Freedom for Palestine." My cheek was quickly covered with a sticky mess. I had been hit in the face with a pie!

Embarrassed and frightened organizers feared I would refuse to continue the widely publicized lecture, but after licking some of the cream from my lips and borrowing a jacket two sizes too large for me, I went onto the stage and said: "I knew that you have a warm and welcoming public, but I didn't know that your cake was so good. I hope it was kosher because I ate quite a lot of it." Everybody laughed and the tension disappeared. The public was clearly on my side even before I started arguing my position. Demonstrations around the hall quickly evaporated.

Generally, my appearances were in fact much more difficult. One typical example was a speech at the University of Amsterdam. There I found myself in a huge overcrowded hall where everyone was as polite as one would expect in Europe. My host was a respectable professor who introduced me properly, read my bio, and then finished with these words: "But of course we all are impatiently waiting for the explanation of how this member of the government which is responsible for committing crimes against humanity is going to talk to us about human rights."

The lecture itself provoked many questions, and when I saw the forest of raised hands I was certain this professor would know whom to call on first. To my great surprise he gave the right of the first question to an old Jew sitting in front of me, whom I had noticed from the beginning and who reminded me of my late father. But my relief was premature. He turned out to be a member of the local Communist Party of Holland and asked me straightaway how I could justify the robbery of Palestine by the people of Israel, and wouldn't it be better for all of us if Israel were banned as a state. The next question was from a sympathetic Palestinian girl who told stories about atrocities committed by Israeli soldiers against her family: rapes, persecutions, prohibitions, expulsions, and her family's narrow escape to Europe. Highly charged personal stories are always the most difficult to respond to. People claim as facts events that are often taken out of context and lack any specifics, let alone any possibility of verification. To dismiss such accusations out of hand seems unfeeling and heartless. And that is the point of such stories.

My usual approach for answering this kind of accusation is to ask questions that might connect the story to some specific event; to ask whether these horrible stories had ever become known to the public; and to remind people of the broader context in which Israel operates. I give numerous examples that show that in a democratic Israel the media, public figures, and politicians openly protest the violation of human rights, and remind the audience that although Israel is caught in a terrible situation of war and mass terror, it insists that human rights be protected, even in the face of mortal questions of security in which the safety of tens and hundreds of lives are at issue.

I remind students of the huge gap between Israel and its enemies when it comes to human rights. This is true for two issues close to the hearts of university students—the rights of women and the rights of homosexuals. Students who are convinced that Israel can do no good and Palestinians, because they are victims who can do no wrong, become confused when I talk about honor killings in Palestinian society, which are widely accepted there. The punishment for such murders is up to six months—a maximum punishment that in fact has never been imposed. I explain that a woman accused of dishonoring her family has a way out, an escape from shame was to become a suicide bomber, for which a special fatwa is given by the spiritual leader of Hamas. I inform students that sometimes knowing the facts of the case may change their sympathies dramatically. An incident in 2003 is a good example. A young Palestinian woman blew herself up at the Karni checkpoint, which allows the passage of goods in and out of Gaza, killing soldiers and civilians as well as herself. She left behind her two children, ages one and three. The Western press suggested her example showed the desperation of the Palestinian people under occupation. But the truth told a different story:

the woman had been accused of unfaithful behavior toward her husband, a Hamas activist, and was to be the victim of an honor killing. The Hamas leader Sheih Yassin then agreed to a special fatwa permitting Hamas to use this woman as a suicide *shahid*. She was given a choice: to die in an honor killing or as a suicide bomber.

Students devoted to human rights are no less troubled when they hear what happens to homosexuals in Palestinian society. The only way for homosexuals in Ramallah or Hebron or Gaza to escape persecution or blackmail or violent assault is to plead for political asylum in Jerusalem. After trying to put the human rights accusations against Israel in a broader context, I ask the students how they can demonstrate on the same day on behalf of rights for women and also on behalf of regimes that systematically trample those rights. I speak about how important it is for me as an Israeli to fight for the right of Palestinians to build a free society not only for humanitarian considerations but as a direct expression of my desire to live in peace and security, which is possible only if all accept and respect human rights, if different identities are recognized and protected and supported. Start fighting, I say, for real freedom and human rights for Palestinians and I will be standing by your side in this struggle.

Fortunately, my speech at Amsterdam University ended rather positively. The representative of the local student's organization told me: You really confused them. Now they aren't sure which side is progressive. Which side is for human rights and democracy, Israelis or Palestinians?

My aim when I lecture at universities is to show the contradiction and collision between these two strange bedfellows: those who believe in human rights and the corrupt dictators and fundamentalists who violate them with impunity. But of course showing that dictators are not their allies is only part of the challenge. You have to try to make clear not only the hypocrisy of the apologists of dictators and terrorists but also the need to fight actively against them.

This is even more difficult because of the debilitating effect of the assault on identity for two generations. Indeed it is hard to persuade those who have already lost their own sense of identity to understand the power identity can have for others. It is hard to give those who don't recognize the importance of defending a particular way of life a reason to defend a particular way of life. And no single lecture, no passionate speech can replace a genuine sense of community, of belonging and commitment to a society, of gaining strength from the bond of identity and democracy. Once this bond exists it proves unbreakable.

A New Beginning in Prague

The Prague conference organized on the initiative of Havel, Aznar, and me in June 2007 brought together a large group of democratic dissidents from many countries across the world: Ethiopia, Russia, China, Belorussia, Libya, Egypt, Syria, Iran, Iraq, and many others. Many had proved their loyalty to the ideas of freedom through years in prisons. Many had been exiled from their countries; and some, even in Prague, had to move under the watchful eyes of their bodyguards. But each of them dreamt not simply of freedom for themselves and their families; their aim was the freedom of their people and their country. Those who were exiled were actively trying to return to their homelands. Those who went back were ready for arrest and oppression. Each had a unique story. Saad a-Din Ibrahim, an Egyptian professor, had spent three years in an Egyptian prison for defending human rights. Released under pressure from the American president, he again confronted the regime. Now he cannot go back. The Lebanese Eli Khoury was an organizer of the enormous demonstration in Beirut against Syrian policies of assassination and undermining of Lebanese sovereignty. Rebiyah Kadeer was a leader of the Uighur people persecuted by the Chinese; both of her sons were in prison. The Palestinian Bassam Aid, the head of a human rights group, every day when he returns to Jericho does not know how that day will end. Gary Kasparov, was also there. He has exchanged his title of world chess champion for the risky position of the leader of the democratic movement in Russia. (When I gave him my book, I inscribed it: To dissident Kasparov from chess player Sharansky.)

While each one spoke to the conference of his different experience, there was a strange feeling that all were telling the same story: the story of the struggle of a free person who threw away the yoke of doublethink and challenged a totalitarian regime. This tale changes clothes and language as it moves from one country to another. It draws on different traditions and different faiths, and gains strength as it connects to others. All of us present at the conference felt as if we had a mutual obligation to defend one another.

In my time in the Gulag, although my fellow prisoners and I each had very different identities, the power of each identity made it possible for us to trust and draw strength from one another. Linking together gave us the energy to resist the vast but dead fields of Communism, where differences were destroyed. In the same way, I felt in Prague that the readiness of each dissident to struggle for the freedom of his or her community was deepened and strengthened by connections and solidarity with the other people around them who also believed in freedom. They were the soldiers in the war of ideas, in which democracy and linked identities face and oppose totalitarianism. And I felt in Prague the power of a truth I learned long ago: When united in a common struggle against evil, the forces of freedom and identity will always triumph.

This is a truth that should be recognized by leaders in the free world because so many problems across the globe have a greater chance of being resolved if we strengthen the alliance between democracy and identity. This alliance is vital for well-established democracies but also for countries making the transition to democracy. When dictatorial rule comes to an end, a formerly repressed identity often springs to the surface. This should not be seen as a threat as long as democracy is taking root at the same time.

When the USSR was falling apart, peoples who had felt themselves to be the victims of forced assimilation for decades, if not centuries, began to insist on their freedom to express their unique identities. The Baltic states, Ukraine, Georgia and many others, demanded independence. Trying to keep the crumbling Soviet Empire together, Mikhail Gorbachev naturally resisted these efforts. Thinking that the emergence of these identities would undermine international peace and stability, the U.S. administration supported him.

But these fears proved unfounded. Framed by democracy, Lithuanian, Ukrainian, Georgian and other nationalisms are a threat to no one. Moreover, by standing with those suppressing identity, the United States missed an opportunity to help these young countries build their democratic institutions and place their emerging democracies on even stronger foundations.

If suppressing identity within an emerging democracy is misguided, so too is ignoring identity. After liberating Iraq from Saddam's tyrannical regime, the U.S.-led coalition failed to realize the fragility of national Iraqi identity. The United States was right to try to establish democracy in Iraq but the effort was undermined when the power of identity was ignored. Extremist fundamentalism, whether Sunni al Qaeda or Shia insurgents from Iran, filled the vacuum. The Shia, Sunni and Kurdish identities in Iraq are very strong. So too are tribal loyalties. Policies that took into account these strong identities—such as the decision in 2006 to work with Sunni tribal leaders in Iraq's Anbar province to fight Al Qaeda—were far more successful than policies that did not. It has become increasingly clear that success in Iraq will ultimately require reconciling freedom and identity by providing sufficient space for the expression of deeply felt religious, ethnic and tribal ties and ensuring that this expression is framed by democracy.

When countries fail to make this reconciliation, peace is endangered. If, as we have seen, democracy without identity invites war, identity without democracy guarantees it.

Saudi Arabia and Iran are threats to peace not because their subjects have strong identities but rather because their regimes permit no democracy. In contrast, the strong identities of the Japanese people endangers no one because of a robust Japanese democracy.

What is true of external peace is true of internal peace. An authoritarian Chinese regime that sees the smallest expression of identity as a threat to its rule brutally represses Tibetans, Uighurs, and others. On the other hand, a democratic India feels no need to repress the scores of vibrant identities within India. The lesson should be clear: Democracy and identity have no problem co-existing when both are strong. We need not choose between them. Only when one or both are weak is there a threat to peace.

The ideal offered by the champions of post-identity of a world without difference is a false one. It is false not only because it will never happen, it is false because the vision it champions is in fact a nightmare. A world without differences is a world that denies people their deepest attachments to history and to the future, to memory and to inheritance. It denies them the things that give life its most profound meaning.

But a society without a strong identity is also a society imperiled. The free world's shield against its enemies is its own identity, vigorously asserted and framed by a commitment to democratic life. Not all cultures are the same. Not all values are equivalent. The right to live a unique way of life is a right worth fighting for and if necessary worth dying for.

United, freedom and identity cannot be defeated. By reconciling these two powerful forces and strengthening this indispensable alliance, we can both fill our lives with purpose and advance the cause of peace.

ACKNOWLEDGMENTS

THIS BOOK IS THE RESULT of the cooperation of two long-time friends, whose families are also friends. For years the ideas discussed in the book were discussed at the shabbat table when the two families came together. The collaboration seemed very natural. However, one challenge emerged from the very beginning. Outside the family discussions, one of us habitually tries to appeal to millions in order to continue his life-long ideological battles; the other writes for a small group of academic specialists. If in the end we have not only finished our project but remained firm friends, it is first of all because of the full support of our families, who patiently and good-humoredly tolerated even our most intense discussions: we want to thank Avital, Rachel, Hanna, Ariel, Tali, Tamar, Eli, and Nomi.

Ron Dermer, who was the co-author of *The Case for Democracy*, this time was serving his country in Washington, D.C., but nevertheless left his imprint. He helped to formulate the book's ideas and edit the manuscript.

The founders of Shalem Center, Yoram Hazony and Dan Polisar, played a very important role in the initial discussions of the project. Vera Golovensky and Roman Polonsky, Natan's colleagues at the Adelson Institute for Strategic Studies, provided valuable input and were a constant source of support. The work of Michael Walzer and his generosity both in sharing ideas and time have been of special importance to Shira Wolosky Weiss, for which she is very grateful.

At different stages the book needed detailed research which was provided by Miriam Friedman, Yair Eldan, Tal Polon, and Diana Feygin.

As with all Natan's previous books, Marvin Josephson offered his professional support as a literary agent and his good counsel as a close friend. Peter Osnos, Natan's long-term partner in crime first in Moscow and then later in publishing, provided indefatigable encouragement, and was well supported by the publishing team at PublicAffairs, led by Susan Weinberg the publisher. Clive Priddle the editorial director, Whitney Peeling the publicity director, and Christine Marra the project editor, worked with intelligence and good humor to make it all happen on time and to overcome the resistance of the authors.

INDEX

PUBLICAFFAIRS is a publishing house founded in 1997. It is a tribute to the standards, values, and flair of three persons who have served as mentors to countless reporters, writers, editors, and book people of all kinds, including me.

I. F. STONE, proprietor of *I. F. Stone's Weekly,* combined a commitment to the First Amendment with entrepreneurial zeal and reporting skill and became one of the great independent journalists in American history. At the age of eighty, Izzy published *The Trial of Socrates,* which was a national bestseller. He wrote the book after he taught himself ancient Greek.

BENJAMIN C. BRADLEE was for nearly thirty years the charismatic editorial leader of *The Washington Post.* It was Ben who gave the *Post* the range and courage to pursue such historic issues as Watergate. He supported his reporters with a tenacity that made them fearless, and it is no accident that so many became authors of influential, best-selling books.

ROBERT L. BERNSTEIN, the chief executive of Random House for more than a quarter century, guided one of the nation's premier publishing houses. Bob was personally responsible for many books of political dissent and argument that challenged tyranny around the globe. He is also the founder and was the longtime chair of Human Rights Watch, one of the most respected human rights organizations in the world.

. . .

For fifty years, the banner of Public Affairs Press was carried by its owner Morris B. Schnapper, who published Gandhi, Nasser, Toynbee, Truman, and about 1,500 other authors. In 1983 Schnapper was described by *The Washington Post* as "a redoubtable gadfly." His legacy will endure in the books to come.

Peter Osnos, *Founder and Editor-at-Large*